Aldous Huxley: a biographical introduction

Leaders of Modern Thought
_____

Series Editor: Christine Bernard

This series is primarily designed for senior school and university students who are studying sociology, history, economics, politics and medicine, yet whose work at some time crosses the disciplines of psychology, literature and philosophy.

The authors writing for this Series, all specialists in their own field, approach the subject of their study from a biographical point of view; they are as concerned with fact as with theory. They introduce the subject's growth, development and discoveries as they relate to his background, family, friends and teachers, within the context of his life, rather than as abstractions of fully-matured theories.

The first three published titles in the Series were NIETZSCHE by Janko Lavrin, SARTRE by Philip Thody and FREUD by Penelope Balogh. Two new studies appear alongside Philip Thody's ALDOUS HUXLEY: KIERKEGAARD by Ronald Grimsley and HO CHI MINH by Charles Fenn. Books in preparation include studies of Kafka, Jung, Trotsky and Camus.

D1634783

Aldous Huxley

a biographical introduction

Philip Thody

Professor of French Literature, University of Leeds

Studio Vista London

By the same author:
Albert Camus. A study of his work (1957)
Jean-Paul Sartre. A literary and political study (1960)
Albert Camus 1913–1960 (1961)
Jean Genet. A study of his novels and plays (1968)
Jean Anouilh (1968)
Laclos: Les Liaisons Dangereuses (1970)

Also in *Leaders of Modern Thought*:
  Sartre: A biographical introduction (1971)

The cover illustration is based on a picture kindly
lent by Messrs Chatto and Windus Ltd

© Philip Thody 1973

Published by Studio Vista
Blue Star House, Highgate Hill, London N19

Set in Times 327 9 on 10 point

Made and Printed in Great Britain by
Richard Clay (Chaucer Press Ltd), Bungay, Suffolk

ISBN 0 289 70189 9 (Hardback)
ISBN 0 289 70188 0 (Paperback)

Contents

To Peter, Caroline, Sarah and Nicholas.

'Like as the arrows in the hand of the giant; even so are the young
children. Happy is the man that hath his quiver full of them; they
shall not be ashamed to speak with their enemies in the gate.'

Psalms, CXXVII, 5–6

Acknowledgements

I am particularly grateful to Mrs Laura Archera Huxley and to
Chatto and Windus for permission to reprint quotations from the
works of Aldous Huxley.

I should like to thank Miss Christine Bernard for the help, advice
and encouragement which she gave me while I was writing this book;
Mrs Allan Gammons, for the exemplary care and patience which
she showed in typing the successive versions and preparing them for
the press; and the Brotherton Library of the University of Leeds
for the calm afforded by its studies, the excellence of its collections,
and the constant helpfulness of its staff.

Once again, my thanks also go to my fellow tax-payers of the United
Kingdom. Their generosity in maintaining large civic universities is
matched only by the freedom they allow to those working in them.

Introduction

Three events dominated the adolescence and early manhood of Aldous Huxley, each of them tragic and each leaving a wound that never completely healed. The first was the death, in November 1908, at the age of 46, of his mother Julia; the second the attack of *keratitis punctata*, in Autumn 1910, which rendered him virtually blind for eighteen months, and left him with his sight permanently impaired; and the third was the suicide, in August 1914, of his elder brother Trevenen. For the external world, as for his own career, it was the second of these three tragedies whose effects were most obvious. He had to give up his ambition to be a doctor, and move away from the world of the biological sciences in which his grandfather, the great Thomas Henry, had achieved such eminence. He devoted himself, instead, to the world of literature and ideas, thus developing a possibility already implicit in the other side of his family tree. Julia Huxley had been the granddaughter of Arnold of Rugby and niece of the poet Matthew Arnold; while her sister, Mrs Humphry Ward, was one of the most successful – and serious – of late Victorian women novelists. In Aldous Huxley, the nineteenth-century impulse towards truth in science and moral values in literature seem in retrospect to have been virtually predestined to mingle by heredity alone. *Keratitis punctata* ensured that the scientific impulse would not predominate; other events had an equally strong influence on the kind of book that Huxley wrote.

The effect which the microbe *staphylococcus pyogenes* chanced to have upon Huxley's eyes seems indeed only to have strengthened an obsession with physical suffering and decay which can be traced back to the impact made on him earlier by the death of his mother. 'She had been good and she had died when he was still a boy; died – but he hadn't been told of that until much later – of creeping and devouring pain. Malignant disease – oh, *caro nome*!' thinks Theodore Gumbril, in *Antic Hay* (1923), while the more openly autobiographical Anthony Beavis, in *Eyeless in Gaza* (1936), is scarred for life by the 'concentrated horror of death' which he undergoes at the age of eleven as he sees the small box containing his mother's ashes being lowered into the 'black well' of her grave.[1] Not one of Huxley's novels is without the obsession of what the flesh can do to the spirit when what man regards as the normal balance of nature is upset. The cancer which killed Julia Huxley is paralleled by the meningitis which tortures little Phil, in *Point Counter Point* (1928), until his wasted body has no defence against death, and this constant presence

of physical disease epitomizes the aspect of the human condition which Huxley the novelist presents most vividly. Man is an animal, and is consequently subject to the impersonal laws governing all forms of life. But, unlike other animals, he has a mind which forces him both to be aware of these biological laws and to reject the amoral, inhuman universe which they reflect. He is appalled by death, suffering and decay, and yet can do nothing, in the last resort, to prevent them conquering. He has, in other words, to live an animal situation in human terms, and a world where 'the greatest tragedy of the spirit is that sooner or later it succumbs to the flesh'[2] is a world in which man is destined to an inevitable defeat.

Noel Trevenen Huxley, the second son of Leonard Huxley and Julia Arnold, was born in 1889, five years before Aldous and two after Julian. He is described by Ronald Clark, in his invaluable *The Huxleys*, as 'perhaps the most gifted of the three omniscient brothers',[3] and he was certainly, if one may judge by photographs, the best looking. His skill and proficiency as a mountaineer suggest that he may also have been the most athletic, and in 1914 the world seemed to lie at his feet. He nevertheless had an experience which, common though it may be for ordinary folk, is most unusual in Huxleys: he secured only second class honours when he took Finals at Oxford. He also failed to secure a place in the Administrative Class of the Civil Service, and this inability to live up to the unremittingly high standards of the Huxley family, occurring at the same time as an unhappy love affair, proved too much for a personality whose inner conflicts were already expressing themselves in a nervous stammer. On 23 August 1914, Noel Trevenen Huxley hanged himself. Aldous wrote at the time that it was 'just the highest and best in Trev – his ideals – which have driven him to his death';[4] and the potentially tragic conflict between ideals and reality is another dominant theme in Huxley's work. Man not only lives in a world where neither his intellect nor his moral conscience can protect him from the casual cruelties of his own body. There is also, within his mind, a perverse demon which constantly makes him act against his own interests, sacrificing his own well-being to the concepts which he himself has forged.

None of the aims which Huxley pursued as a writer was unconnected with these early experiences. Had his eyesight been better, he might well have followed a career in the experimental sciences, or found some other calling in the field of learning or administration. He would then almost certainly not have had to write books to earn money, and his reputation in literary circles might well stand higher today if he had not felt compelled to be so productive. From a more intellectual point of view, both the iconoclasm and the mistrust of conventional social values are undoubtedly linked to his brother's suicide. Ideas, he suggests, especially if they demand the sacrifice of our instincts to our intellect, are very dangerous. Man's ability to talk, to elaborate complex intellectual notions, to define abstract ideas to the point where they acquire an independent existence, constantly tends to alienate him from his own true interests. This is as true of sex as it is of religion or politics, and the plea for tolerance and agnosticism running through the whole of Huxley's work gives it both its unity and its permanent appeal.

Huxley was, however, less successful in providing a satisfactory course to the problems made acute for him by his mother's death. His fundamental aim as a writer was always to make sense of his own experience, and initially he tried to do this through literature itself. Life might have no meaning, but the artist could at least impose some significant pattern upon experience by recasting it in an aesthetically satisfying form. Then, largely under the influence of D. H. Lawrence, he attempted to argue that man could best deal with the aberrations of his own mind by striving to recapture, in his actual behaviour, some of the harmony attained in other civilizations. When, for a variety of reasons this attempt to revitalize paganism proved a disappointment, he entered his third and final stage: the one where he argued that man's ultimate end was revealed to him by certain types of mystical experiences. He thus exemplified, in the expression which his books gave to his own evolution as a thinker, three of the major responses which human beings can make to the world in which they find themselves: the aesthetic, the humanistic and the religious. Yet at no stage did he overcome the scandal of undeserved physical suffering, and his attempt to reconcile science and mysticism remains, in this respect, a splendid failure.

The ideas which Huxley discussed in his work also have an intrinsic interest which is by no means always linked to his own problems, and he certainly knew more science than any other imaginative writer of his generation. His discussion of the impact of science on society is particularly interesting, irrespective of any relationship that this may or may not have had with his own private experience, and the same is true of his views on the relationship between science and literature, on ethics, on religion, on the role of the individual in history, on drugs, overpopulation, pacifism, and the possibilities of unorthodox medicine. Even his sternest critics acknowledge both Huxley's 'flair for embodying the Zeitgeist' and his skill as a 'populariser of ideas' and there can still be few more stimulating, painless and more amusing ways of introducing oneself to the problems which occupied literate Europeans and Americans between 1920 and 1960 than to read his novels and essays. Neither are these the only reasons for including a biographical introduction to Aldous Huxley in a series entitled 'Leaders of Modern Thought'. When the most intelligent inheritor of a brilliant scientific tradition becomes a mystic, we need to revise our defence of the way we live now, and of the values on which we try to base our civilization. This defence becomes even more interesting to make as we come to realize that Huxley's later philosophy of religion continues to reflect, albeit in an unexpected and not always convincing manner, two of the attitudes which most characterize the scientific outlook: a positivistic respect for facts and an intense distrust of metaphysics.

1 Education and a career

Aldous Huxley was born at Laleham, Sussex, on 26 July 1894, into what his cousin Gervas later called the 'well-to-do intellectual upper middle-class in what was then the greatest and wealthiest country in the world'.[1] At the age of seven and a half, he went to the mixed school which his mother had just founded at Prior's Field, also in Sussex, but as soon as he was nine his education began to conform to the established customs of his class. In 1903 he went to a boys' preparatory school called Hillside, and at the age of thirteen followed his brothers Julian and Trevenen to Eton.

Sometimes, and especially in his later years, Huxley could be very critical of his schooling. 'Looking back over my own education,' he wrote in 1956, 'I can see the enormous deficiencies of a system which could do nothing better for my body than Swedish drill and compulsory football, nothing better for my character than prizes, punishments, sermons and pep talks, and nothing better for my soul than hymns at bed-time, to the accompaniment of a harmonium';[2] and this view of his schooldays is well within the normal pattern for English upper middle-class intellectuals. Gervas Huxley, six months his senior, remembers him 'weeping copiously' during his first day at Hillside, and Aldous was constitutionally quite unsuited to the lack of privacy, the bullying, and the general rough-and-tumble of an English boarding school. He had been a delicate child, slow in learning to walk, and uninterested in the kind of violent games which were the only suitable preparation for life at Hillside. Yet it was, as Gervas wrote, 'impossible to have a quarrel with him', and the 'deeply interested curiosity' with which Huxley even then surveyed the world about him served as a kind of protection against its brutalities. At the age of five, asked by an aunt what he was thinking about so intensely, Aldous had turned and uttered one word: 'skin'.[3] His education at least had the negative virtue of not destroying his curiosity, and when, in his middle 'humanist' period, he thought about it in social rather than intellectual terms, he showed a surprising appreciation of what it had had to offer.

Thus when discussing, in 1929, the upbringing best suited to the needs of the human type which he then regarded as most admirable, the 'life-worshipper', Huxley remarked that it could be best obtained by 'the most conventional of gentlemanly and Anglican public school educations'. This would need to be followed at the University, he added, by 'an intensive course of theoretical Pyrrhonism and the practice of Blake's most subversive precepts', but the life-worshipper's 'public school traditions' would nevertheless bring him 'honourably and sensibly through the affairs of social life' and thus lay solid foundations for the more important business of living fully, intensely and harmoniously. Three years later, in 1932, Huxley even had something to say in favour of games. 'Battles may still be won on the playing fields of Eton', he wrote in *Beyond the Mexique Bay*, 'but what is perhaps more creditable to those elm-shadowed expanses of soggy turf, colonial empires are humanely lost there', and he went on – in curious anticipation of the events of the nineteen-fifties – to stress the advantages which cricket and scepticism had given to the English in the difficult task of losing their empire.[4] Although he lived the last third of his life almost exclusively in California, where many of his ideas became increasingly more unusual as he explored the worlds of unorthodox medicine, mysticism and mescalin, Huxley nevertheless remained in many ways intensely English. In particular, he never lost his upper middle-class English accent, and he noted in 1949, on hearing a recording of himself reading passages from his own books, how little that accent itself had changed in the last hundred years.

'Language is perpetually changing', he wrote, 'the cultivated English I listened to as a child is not the same as the cultivated English spoken by young men and women to-day. But within the general flux there are islands of linguistic conservatism; and when I listen to myself objectively, from the outside, I perceive that I am one of these islands. In the Oxford of Jowett and Lewis Carroll, the Oxford in which my mother was brought up, how did people speak the Queen's English? I can answer with a considerable degree of confidence that they spoke almost exactly as I do. These recordings of 1950 are at the same time documents from the seventies and eighties of the last century.'[5]

Huxley was still at Hillside when his mother died in November 1908, and the chapters in *Eyeless in Gaza* in which Anthony Beavis returns to his preparatory school, Bulstrode, after his mother's funeral are the most autobiographical in the whole of Huxley's fiction. Even the description of how Brian Foxe tries to console Anthony by sailing the little boat he had made in the school carpenter's shop along the gutter outside their dormitory is based upon reality, and Huxley once again expressed a fairly appreciative attitude towards his schooling when he told his second wife, Laura Archera Huxley, how useful he thought it was that boys should be given the chance to make their own toys in this way.[6] Eton must none the less have seemed more congenial than Hillside to a boy of Aldous's temperament, even if only for the greater degree of privacy which it afforded, and he seems to have been reasonably happy there.

According to Gervas Huxley, however, it was the authorities at Eton who were at least partly to blame for the severity of the disease which blinded him in Autumn 1910. 'When run down after influenza and out on a field day with the Eton OTC,' he writes, 'a streptococcus infection from dust attacked his eyes. Had penicillin been discovered it would, no doubt, have cleared the whole thing up in a short time, but as it was, the Eton authorities neglected his condition and he had almost completely lost the sight of both eyes before my father was informed and brought him to London to see specialists.'[7]

It is often under stress that our true personality stands out most clearly, and it was during the period of total blindness which afflicted him between the ages of sixteen and seventeen that some of Huxley's most attractive characteristics revealed themselves. He was totally without self-pity, and immediately applied himself to learning Braille. It did, he wrote to his cousin Gervas, have the great advantage of enabling one to read in bed without taking one's hands out from under the blankets. Music was also an activity which Huxley could still follow, and in June 1912 he went to Marburg, in Switzerland, in order both to pursue this interest and improve his knowledge of German. Eventually, his sight did improve to the point where, as he said in *The Art of Seeing* in 1942, he had 'one eye just capable of light perception, and the other with enough vision to permit of detecting the two-hundred-foot letter on the Snellen Chart at ten feet' and he was able to indulge again in what he once described as his favourite vice: voracious and indiscriminate reading.[8] It was an activity that was to be immediately relevant both to his University studies and to the literary journalism upon which he depended, for the earlier part of his career at least, for a good deal of his income.

Huxley's opinion of the class into which he had been born differed in at least one respect from that of his cousin Gervas, in so far as he personally was never conscious of its wealth. Indeed, he described himself in *Jesting Pilate*, in 1926, as belonging to that 'impecunious but dignified section of the upper middle-class which is in the habit of putting on dress-clothes to eat – with the most studied decorum and out of porcelain and burnished silver – a dinner of dishwater and codfish, mock duck and cabbage', and neither he nor any of the autobiographical characters in his novels was ever to display that self-confidence in dealing with other people that stems from membership of a class conscious of its wealth and power.[9] Concepts of poverty are none the less essentially relative. To move from a preparatory school to Eton and from Eton to Oxford does not actually betoken a family on the bread-line, and it is perhaps again significant, in this respect, that none of the major characters in Huxley's fiction is ever seriously short of money. Neither is any of them a failure in his chosen profession, and Huxley's career at Balliol, which he entered in 1913, the year in which his brother

Julian graduated with first-class honours in Zoology, was a prefiguration of the brilliance with which he was to make his mark in
the literary world of the nineteen-twenties. His rooms became the
centre for the liveliest and most interesting people, and his readiness
to anticipate rather than follow popular taste was visible both in his
liking for rag-time, which he strummed enthusiastically on an old,
upright piano, and in the large French travel poster 'depicting a
group of nubile nude girls by a sea-shore' which he pinned above his
mantlepiece. He did not, however, think highly of the diet offered
by the University authorities, and wrote scathingly of the Finals
Papers which, by their neglect of any topics that could not be treated
from textbooks, degraded Oxford 'to the level of the third-class
colonial cram-book-colleges'.[10]

Huxley's contempt for his Finals Papers did not, however, prevent
him from receiving First-Class Honours when he graduated in
English literature in June 1916, and it is quite extraordinary to the
modern reader of works such as *Text and Pretexts* that he did not
go straight into University teaching. However, as he wrote to
Juliette Baillot, his brother Julian's fiancée, in November 1918, the
English School at Oxford was 'too impoverished to pay the men it
already possesses', and he was obliged instead to take a job as a
master at Eton. He was not outstandingly successful with any but
the most intelligent pupils, but an indication of the level at which
both he – and his colleagues – worked can be found in Cyril
Connolly's recollection that the Frenchman responsible for teaching
modern languages had to refer constantly to Huxley's English translation of Mallarmé's *Après-midi d'un faune* in order to find out what
the original French of the poem meant. The boredom which
Theodore Gumbril, in *Antic Hay* (1923), felt when confronted with
an apparently unending series of essays all containing the phrase
about Pope Pius IX being 'a good man but of less than average
intelligence' doubtless reflects something of the impatience which
Huxley felt at schoolmastering, but not all the passages in this novel
are equally autobiographical. 'You gave me a pedagogue's education' Gumbril tells his father, 'and then washed your hands of me',
and even as late as 1950 the reproach struck John Wain as sufficiently
valid as a general comment on the Arts Faculties in English Universities for him to include it in a critical account of his own career.[11]
Huxley's purely literary education, however, was not a sin which he
could lay at his father's door, since his own poor eyesight put any
career involving practical experimentation in science quite out of the
question. He did, it is true, work for a brief spell at the Air Ministry
in 1918, and once again translated his experience into a rather
disillusioned piece of fiction. In *Those Barren Leaves* (1925), Francis
Chellifer works for a time at the Air Board, 'haggling with German
Jews over the price of chemicals and celluloid, with Greek brokers

over the castor oil, with Ulstermen over the linen', and comes to realize that a life in commerce or industry, where he will work hard 'in order that Jewish stockbrokers may exchange their Rovers for Armstrong-Siddeleys' is definitely not for him.[12]

As far as one can tell from his letters, Huxley himself never even considered the possibility of going into either business or administration, and it is interesting to compare his career in this respect with that of his cousin Gervas, whose ability to fit into the modern world contrasts so markedly with Aldous's automatic rejection of anything but a life devoted to literature and ideas. After a distinguished war record, in which he won the Military Cross, Gervas went first of all into private business and subsequently into public relations, first on behalf of the Tea Marketing Board and then of the Empire Marketing Board. Like Julian Huxley, who was knighted in 1961 for services both to science and to administration, Gervas ended his career with the customary inclusion in the Honours List, becoming a C.M.G. in 1954, and Huxley's attitude towards society gives a very one-sided account of how members of his class and family tended to behave. Like many other English and American writers of his time, Huxley also lived much of his life abroad, and this additional separation from the day to day responsibilities and concerns of his fellow countrymen undoubtedly influenced both the portrait which he drew of modern society and the philosophical conclusions at which he eventually arrived. It is true that Huxley never expressed regret for this exclusion from the active world, and seemed at times even to delight in it. Philip Quarles, his self-portrait in *Point Counter Point* (1928), rejoices as he drives down Whitehall in the system that enables him to delegate responsibility for running the world's affairs to other people, and none of the characters in Huxley's major novels has a job which requires him to turn up regularly at the office or take responsibility for commercial or administrative decisions. Yet while this absence of regular employment brought Huxley the freedom which he prized most dearly as the great advantage of the writer's calling, it did mean that he was, especially in the early part of his career, conscious of what his grandfather had also had occasion to call 'all the abominable anxieties which attend a fluctuating income'.[13] This, in turn, had an impact both upon his relationship with his father and the frequency with which he produced certain types of books.

ii

Both as an undergraduate and during his brief spells at Eton and the Air Ministry, Huxley made frequent visits to Garsington manor, the country house where Lady Ottoline Morrell played hostess to many of the leading intellectuals of her day. Bertrand Russell was a frequent visitor, as was also the young Lytton Strachey, who later remembered Huxley – not very kindly – as being 'incredibly cultured', but 'looking like a piece of seaweed'. Garsington did not, however, merely provide Huxley with the setting for what Angus Wilson called the 'Country House Novels'[14] and the models for some of the intellectuals portrayed in *Crome Yellow* (1920) or *Those Barren Leaves*. It was also there that he met and fell in love with his future wife, a young Belgian girl of fine and delicate beauty called Maria Nys. With no job, and no immediate prospect of finding one, Huxley was able to marry and set up home only with the help of a loan made to him by his father, and one to be 'repaid punctiliously over the years'.[15] The marriage took place on 10 July 1919, and their son, Matthew, was born in April of the following year.

It was undoubtedly Leonard Huxley's misfortune to have been a man of considerable competence in a family of extraordinary brilliance. The biographical tribute which he paid to his father in *The Life and Letters of T. H. Huxley* remains the best introduction to the man who styled himself as 'Darwin's bulldog', and who did more than anyone else to popularize and extend scientific knowledge and education in nineteenth-century England; while the contribution which he made to the general cultural life of the country by his editorship of *The Cornhill Magazine*, as well as by his work for the publishing house of Macmillan, would have been more than a reasonable life's work for most ordinary men. As it is, however, Leonard Huxley is not only a person whose achievements inevitably seem very modest when compared to those of his brilliant father and his two equally brilliant sons. He is also, for anyone in the least acquainted with Aldous Huxley's novels, so obviously the model for the pedantic and uxorious John Beavis in *Eyeless in Gaza* (1936) that it is difficult to regard him as a person who led what was by most normal standards a happy and successful life. It may well be true, as Gervas Huxley remarks, that he was 'never much help' to Aldous, and his passion for mountaineering, coupled with what Ronald Clark describes as the habit of 'retaining schoolboy interests past middle age', certainly helped to separate him from a son who never showed much enthusiasm for the Alpine scene and who struck all observers as preternaturally adult.[16] Yet by no stretch of the imagination can Leonard Huxley have been as bad as the John Beavis of *Eyeless in Gaza*, and he undoubtedly suffered from Huxley's need to find the models for the characters in his novels from among his own family and circle of friends.

There may also, of course, have been subconscious motives at work in determining the hostility which Huxley reveals, throughout his fiction, towards the man whom he always addressed in his letters as 'Dearest father'. To a Freudian, it would be quite obvious that Huxley's adoration of his mother implied feelings of intense jealousy for his father, and that these were translated into the subconscious notion that Leonard Huxley was at least partly guilty for his wife's death. A thorough-going Freudian would also see the hostility which Huxley always shows for Freud's ideas as an indication of the fear which he had that such a diagnosis might be true, and the fact that almost all the fathers in Huxley's fiction are caricatures would lend weight to this view. Yet there are other, more easily acceptable ideological reasons for the hostile portraits of fathers in Huxley's early fiction. In *Those Barren Leaves*, Francis Chellifer's father considers 'a walk among the mountains as the equivalent of church going', and suggests one Easter morning that he and his son should climb to the top of Snowdon. When they reach the summit, he contemplates the view with no comment other than 'Bloody fine', before interrupting the long and otherwise totally silent descent with a sudden and unexplained recital of a passage from Wordsworth's *Prelude*. Francis Chellifer's later realization, under the influence of the early Wittgenstein, that the Wordsworthian formulae in which his father so evidently believed were 'as meaningless as so many hiccoughs'[17] is a particularly good example of the appeal which Huxley's revolt against Victorianism made to his readers in the nineteen-twenties. It was up to date, and even slightly in advance of intellectual fashion. The *Tractatus Logico-Philosophicus*, from which the remark about hiccoughs was obviously taken, had not been published until 1920, only five years before *Those Barren Leaves*, and Wittgenstein was still known only to a small circle of initiates. Moreover, it was directed against figures in whom Huxley's contemporaries could see their own fathers as well as those who had been responsible for the outbreak and senseless prolongation of the first world war, and thus had an emotional as well as an ideological appeal. Yet Huxley's rejection of the moral and spiritual values of his father's generation did not stem only from differences of personal temperament and intellectual fashion. Sex and money came into it as well, and the impact on his fiction of this aspect of Huxley's relationship with his father is suspiciously easy to detect in so self-conscious and intelligent an artist.

Thus one of the few psychological themes in *Eyeless in Gaza* on which Huxley does not himself make a specific comment is the contrast between the refusal or inability of the central character, Anthony Beavis, to settle down in married life, and the speed with which his father recovers from his grief at the death of his deeply loved first wife and marries 'a rather plump and snubbily pretty young woman of seven and twenty'.[18] Less than five years after the death of Julia Huxley, Leonard Huxley also married again, and Rosalind Bruce, his second wife, was less than half his own age. Although there is no evidence that the grief which Leonard Huxley experienced when Aldous's mother died, and which inspired him to

B

write a poem that he recited to the assembled pupils at Prior's Field on the day immediately following Julia Huxley's death, had quite the same therapeutic effect as John Beavis's positively self-indulgent mourning rites, his second marriage must inevitably have seemed, in the eyes of his son, something of a betrayal. It did not, fortunately, prevent Aldous from making a very happy marriage, but it undoubtedly affected his portrayal of marriage and of fathers both in *Eyeless in Gaza* and in his other novels. This second marriage also meant, apparently, that the £40,000 left to Leonard Huxley by his first wife had to be used to educate the two sons which he later had by Rosalind Bruce, and could be made available only on fairly impersonal financial terms to his children by his first marriage.[19]

It is of course true that no father can be expected to support his children indefinitely. Nevertheless, the intensity with which Aldous threw himself into journalism in order to provide for his wife and son later became what D. H. Lawrence clearly thought was something of an obsession with money,[20] and a preoccupation which a more generous distribution of Julia's property might perhaps have avoided. In April 1920, Huxley took a job as dramatic critic with the *Westminster Gazette*, thus making himself undergo what he later presented as the rather depressing experience of seeing some two hundred and fifty plays a year, and also wrote articles on a wide variety of subjects for Condé Nast in *House and Garden*. He even composed advertising copy and other articles for *Vogue*, and commented later on the valuable lessons which could be learned by having to write articles likely to persuade people to buy things. He was a good journalist, who took pleasure both in his ability to communicate with his readers and in the opportunities which this provided for earning a living, but perhaps inevitably the quality of his purely literary work suffered. Hardly a year went by without his publishing either a novel or a book of essays, and his output led Cyril Connolly to remark ironically, in 1930, that 'the first forty years of Aldous Huxley's literary career have been marred by overproduction, for which the present economic climate is to blame.'[21] Less charitably, a critic writing in T. S. Eliot's highly Anglican review *The Criterion*, dismissed Huxley in 1931 as a 'literary journalist', who has 'heard everything and thought about nothing'. Moreover, added 'M.B.' (probably Montgomery Belgion), because most of the essays in *Music at Night* 'appeared originally in *Vanity Fair*, the American magazine for smart people', Huxley deserved consideration neither as a writer nor as a thinker.[22]

The ferocity of these remarks is paralleled, thirty-three years later, by the bland comment, in *The Year's Work in English Studies* for 1964, that Huxley had been 'dismissed as a novelist in the early nineteen-fifties',[23] and the treatment which professional critics of English literature have meted out to him is one of the more interesting minor aspects of his career. For although it seems, to his non-literary admirers, yet another sign of the effect which the existence of two cultures, one literary and the other scientific, has upon the reputation of authors who use fiction to popularize and exploit scientific ideas, it is for the literary man a thoroughly justified result of the greater rigour brought into English studies by the Leavisite revolution. Huxley certainly regretted the need to write quickly, and told his brother Julian, during the composition of *Point Counter Point* in 1927, how much he envied the opportunity which Flaubert had enjoyed of devoting five years of his life to the writing of *Madame Bovary*.[24] It was nevertheless when he was writing under financial pressure, in the early part of his career, that he produced his most aesthetically satisfying novels, and the deleterious effect which his journalism is sometimes held to have had on the quality of his work is restricted to his essays. Whatever resentment he may have felt with his sub-conscious mind for the financial effects which his father's second marriage had on his career, this had no long-term effect upon his personal relationships. In March 1934, after his father's death, he offered to help pay for the education of his two half-brothers, David and Andrew.[25]

2 The patterns of satire

Huxley actually began his literary career as a poet, and continued to make occasional use of verse even in his later novels. His first book of poems, *The Burning Wheel*, was published by Basil Blackwell in 1916, and was followed in 1918 by *The Defeat of Youth and other poems*. From the very beginning of his career, Huxley kept excellent literary company, appearing in the first number of the magazine *Arts and Letters* alongside Richard Aldington, Siegfried Sassoon and Wyndham Lewis, and he remarked later that he never had any difficulty in finding a publisher for his work. In his contribution to the *Memorial Volume* edited by Sir Julian Huxley in 1964, the year after Aldous's death, T. S. Eliot nevertheless remarked that he himself had been 'unable to show any enthusiasm' for Huxley's verse, and it is perhaps significant that the poem which has best stood the test of time should also deal with the themes which gave his fiction its originality and immediate appeal: science, sex, and the extraordinary oddness of human life.[1]

> A million million spermatozoa,
>   All of them alive:
> Out of their cataclysm but one poor Noah
>   Dare hope to survive.
>
> And among that million minus one
>   Might have chanced to be
> Shakespeare, another Newton, a new Donne –
>   But the One was Me.
> Shame to have ousted your betters thus,
>   Taking ark while the others remained outside!
> Better for all of us, forward Homunculus,
>   If you'd quietly died!

This poem, the *Fifth Philosopher's Song*, was first published in 1920, and Huxley's use of scientific knowledge to make philosophical points typified not only his early novels but also the conversation with which he entertained his friends. 'He preferred to discourse,' writes Sir Osbert Sitwell, describing a visit which Huxley paid him in 1919, 'of some erudite and impersonal scandals, such as the incestuous mating of melons, the elaborate love-making of lepidoptera, or the curious amorous habits of cuttlefish', and Roy Campbell has similar but less kindly recollections of a Huxley who 'leeringly gloated over his knowledge of how crayfish copulated'.[2] In Huxley's novels, however, the scandals were less impersonal, and it was indeed the case, as Mark Rampion was to put it in *Point Counter Point*, that the higher the brow, the lower the loins.[3] The immediate appeal of *Crome Yellow*, *Antic Hay* and *Those Barren Leaves* undoubtedly stems from the sophisticated tone with which Huxley links sexual immorality with scientific knowledge, but this is by no means their only attraction. These three novels all have something of the quality which D. H. Lawrence affected to despise in the Greek philosophers when he wrote in the first version of *Lady Chatterley's Lover* of 'the excitement which they got out of argument, and reason and thought'. 'They're awfully like little boys', Lawrence made Sir Clifford continue, 'who have just discovered that they can think and are beside themselves about it. They're so thrilled that nothing else matters, only thinking and knowledge'.[4] Although this description was only accidentally appropriate, the influence which D. H. Lawrence subsequently had over Huxley certainly owed much to the contrast which his more powerfully emotional work and personality provided. Indeed, one of the permanent features of Huxley's character was a desire to go beyond the extreme intellectuality which came so naturally to him, and it was the example of Lawrence which initially made this possible for him.

Huxley did, however, draw one very firm moral conclusion from the medley of ideas which, even as late as the nineteen-forties, made the reading of his early novels such an intellectually exciting experience. It might well be true, as Mr Scogan argued after dinner at Crome, that we differ from the rest of the animal kingdom in being wholly unpredictable. Since we are not, unlike the animals and plants, wholly determined by our heredity and environment, we cannot be certain what we shall become. It may be that, in the Caesarean environment of the twentieth century, the potential Neros or Caligulas which we all carry within us will come to fruition. On the other hand, they may not, and we may – through no merit of our own – live a life of perfect virtue. But whatever happens, and whatever vices and virtues the curious mixture of freedom and determinism that characterize mankind reveals as lying within us, there is one thing we must not do. We must never allow our intellectual convictions to bring us to the point where we agree to kill our fellow men. It may well be that we live in an unpredictable world, in which 'the microbe *staphylococcus pyogenes* produces in some places boils, in others sties in the eye' and where it is even responsible 'in certain cases, for *keratitis punctata*'.[5] What we must not do is either expect reality to fit our ideas or attempt to force it into a preconceived mould. It may perhaps be true, as the Freudians allege, that Filippo Lippi is 'an incestuous homosexualist with a bent towards anal-eroticism' and it is certainly the case that, in sexual matters, 'some people like blood. And some like boots. And some like long gloves and corsets. And some like birch rods. And some like sliding down slopes and can't look at Michelangelo's "Night" on the Medici tombs without dying the little death.'[6] What is equally certain is that we live in a world where no belief compels actions, especially in the field of religion and politics.

It is noticeable, in this respect, that there is only one character in Huxley's first three novels who is wholly obnoxious. He appears in *Crome Yellow* and is the Anglican vicar, Mr Bodiham, the 'iron man' who 'beats with a flail on the souls of his congregation' in an attempt to convince them that the casualties of the first world war are as much part of God's Eternal Plan as the bloodshed foretold in Matthew, xxix, 7, or in the sixteenth chapter of the Revelations of St John the Divine.[7] Even before his official sponsorship of pacifism in 1936, Huxley was acutely aware of the harm produced by nonsense of this kind, and his awareness was more often than not couched in terms which, like so many other ideas in his first three novels, seemed deliberately calculated to make their greatest appeal to the iconoclastic and highly sexed young. What injustice, declared Mr Cardan in *Those Barren Leaves*, what monstrous unfairness, that the moralists of the nineteenth century should have succeeded in limiting 'the connotation of the word "immoral" in such a way that, for practical purposes, only those were immoral who drank too much or made too copious love'.[8] Those who indulged in the more dangerous vices of political cruelty or righteous indignation, he continued, were thus able to escape scot-free, and this theme of how superior hedonism is to patriotism or religious fervour is a theme that recurs time and again in Huxley's work. Philip Quarles, in *Point Counter Point*, remarks that he has discovered the only true basis for a League of Nations when an itinerant Arab uses all the known European languages in an attempt to sell him dirty postcards, and Huxley never tired of insisting that it was less harmful to talk about the God of Brothels than about the God of Battles.[9]

What distinguishes Huxley, however, is his awareness that this rejection of past beliefs because of the suffering they have caused also involves a subversion of all traditional moral values. If one limited oneself to results, private vices might well be preferable to public virtues; and if this were the case, then the whole emphasis which Catholics, Protestants and humanists had placed not only upon chastity and thrift but also upon loyalty and courage was a complete mistake. Huxley set out, in other words, from the presupposition that God either did not exist or that He did not concern himself with the affairs of this world; and drew from this idea the conclusion that there was no basis other than a purely pragmatic one for judging human behaviour. He consequently had to recognize – and appeared at first sight to take great delight in so doing – that if sensuality did less harm than patriotism or religious belief, it was morally preferable.

It is nevertheless here that the first major contradiction in Huxley's work makes itself felt. Neither the behaviour nor the achievements of the characters in *Crome Yellow*, *Antic Hay* or *Those Barren Leaves* ever suggests that pleasure seeking or sexual indulgence can make people either happy or good; and Huxley's early novels give the curious impression of having been written by a twentieth-century thinker working out his intellectual conclusions within the framework of an emotional preference for monogamy, romantic love, and high moral principles which is almost Victorian in its intensity. This instinctive rejection of nihilism is, of course, well within the Huxley tradition, and constitutes one of the many similarities between Aldous Huxley and his grand-father. When, in 1860, his four-year-old son Noel died of scarlet fever, Thomas Henry Huxley went out of his way, in a letter to Charles Kingsley, to reject St Paul's words: 'If the dead rise not again, let us eat and drink, for tomorrow we die'. 'Why,' he wrote, 'the very apes know better, and if you shoot their young, grieve their grief out and do not immediately seek distraction in a gorge.'[10] The tone in which Aldous Huxley describes the sexual antics of his characters both in *Those Barren Leaves* and in *Brave New World* (1932) leaves no doubt that he shared his grand-father's revulsion against any abandonment of personal morality, and it is curious to note how even the biological framework for his pessimism echoes a nineteenth-century dilemma. For as Huxley himself suggested, albeit rather ironically, the *Fifth Philosopher's Song* is only a restatement in more scientifically accurate terms of the concern which Tennyson expresses over the reality of Divine Providence when he notes, in *In Memoriam*, how out of fifty seeds, God 'often brings but one to life'; and in one of his own apparently less serious moods, Thomas Henry Huxley commented to Charles Darwin in 1871 how odd it was that a person might fall victim to insanity because his '*nth* ancestor had lived between tide marks'.[11] But if Aldous Huxley was by no means the first to be conscious of the incompatibility between scientific determinism and the views of those who

'trusted God was love indeed,
And love creation's final law.'

there was nevertheless an important difference between the kind of science with which Aldous Huxley was confronted and the kind which his grandfather had done so much to propagate.

For Thomas Henry Huxley's contemporaries, scientific materialism did at least appear to offer a viable alternative to Christianity. Matter was real, measurable, a reliable basis on which to order both the organization of society and our knowledge of the world. For Aldous Huxley, however, acquainted as he was with the views of Planck and Einstein, matter had lost its old, enviable solidity, and the physical world in which man had to face his personal, moral or political problems was just as disconcertingly complex as the maze of philosophical or ethical notions in which he had been cast by the disappearance of religious belief. How, asks Calamy in *Those Barren Leaves* – discussing the question, appropriately enough, with his mistress in bed – should he go about giving a correct description of his hand? Should he see it as a physicist would, as an 'almost inconceivable number of atoms, each consisting of a greater or lesser number of units of negative electricity whirling several times round a nucleus of positive electricity'? Or should he see it as a chemist, stressing the number of architectural patterns into which the molecules are built? Or as a biologist, seeing its complicated cell-structure? Or as a moralist, emphasizing its role as an instrument capable of performing good or bad acts? Or as an *homme moyen sensuel*, appreciating first and foremost its ability to feel pain or pleasure and to express love or hate? For within its context, observes Calamy, each of these ways is sufficient and is accurate. But the descriptions of the scientist are so different from those of the moralist that the object itself completely changes its nature, and even among the scientists themselves there is no agreement about what constitutes the 'real' hand. As soon as we begin to think about man's place in nature and the meaning of our own experience, 'gulfs begin opening up around you – more and more abysses, as though the ground were splitting in an earthquake.'[12] Compared to philosophy, politics or theology, science is man's most successful intellectual enterprise. He can, within certain definable limits, make statements that are susceptible of being proved right or wrong, and can apply science to produce, in many cases, mathematically predictable and financially profitable results. But when science itself presents him, in relation to his own body and to the hand which has given him mastery over the rest of nature, with a picture of reality which is like the smile on the face of the Cheshire cat, inexplicable in origin and yet remaining present when its apparent support has been taken away, the possibility of coming up with any answers at all in the more difficult realms of religion, ethics or political philosophy becomes infinitely remote.

It is no doubt tempting, within the framework of contemporary English philosophy, to dismiss Calamy's problem as meaningless. Huxley makes him talk like this, it could be argued, only because both he and his character have begun by expecting science to do something quite impossible: give an account of reality in terms of an anthropocentric philosophy which expects everything to be explicable in the most rudimentary terms of causation, necessity and function. It is, on the contrary, part of the very nature of the world to be complex and many-sided; and to imagine that any single picture of reality will tell the whole truth is as foolishly naïve as to expect that a reading of the college accounts will indicate how undergraduates study Anglo-Saxon or attend the May ball. Gilbert Ryle's essay on *The World of Science and the everyday world*[13] points out the futility of the approach to science implicit in Calamy's lament, and a brief analysis of the way in which language works is enough to show us that Calamy – and Huxley through him – has been crying for the moon. Each set of concepts is valid on its own ground. Let us leave it at that, and not require a biologist to answer questions about right and wrong that should never have been addressed to him in the first place.

In the broader context of man's attempt to find meaning in his life, and especially in his own and other people's suffering, Calamy's question nevertheless does become philosophically valid. For all the courage and good humour with which he personally bore adversity and illness, Huxley could never move to the stage where he looked with equanimity at a universe whose impersonal laws seemed at times deliberately to thwart the human quest for meaning. It was not that he expected the whole universe to revolve around man. Like his grandfather, he accepted the view that man is a part of nature, not the centre. But just as Thomas Henry Huxley had been forced, through the death of his son Noel, to confront the impossibility of living in human terms a life constantly at the mercy of biological accidents, so Aldous Huxley had been compelled, by his own personal tragedies as well as through the experience of his generation, to realize how man's analysis of the world through science often only heightened the irony of his impotence to control or even to understand it. There might perhaps be some slightly perverse intellectual satisfaction to be derived from writing of someone dying of cancer, as Huxley does in his very last novel, *Island*, that 'a little piece of her body began to obey the second law of thermodynamics'.[14] But at no point in the forty-five years of Huxley's literary career can his anguish be dispelled either by scientific notions or linguistic analysis.

This subjection of man to the unpredictable whims of the physical universe is, however, treated in several different ways in Huxley's fiction, not all of them uniformly solemn. Two short stories, in particular, *The Farcical History of Richard Greenow* (1920) and *The Claxtons* (1930), stand out as much by their humour as well as by the general questions which they raise. The second, moreover, with its portrait of an upper-middle-class family in which 'brewery almost infallibly leads to impressionism or theosophy or communism' shows Huxley at his best as a social satirist while also putting forward a view about the upbringing of children which even nowadays is unusual among English literary intellectuals. There might, it suggests, be a good deal to be said in favour of conventional

behaviour and common sense, and this is borne out by the plot. For
when Sylvia Claxton is temporarily released from the impeccably
progressive atmosphere of her home, where life is 'one long *risorgi-
mento* against forgiving Austrians and all too gently smiling
Bourbons', she suddenly discovers happiness: if she wishes to play
with other children, she has to 'adapt herself to democracy and
parliamentary government', and Huxley's basic fondness for democracy shows itself quite clearly in the metaphors he uses.[15] Unfortunately, however, this idyllic excursion into reality does not last.
Sylvia has to go back to the mother who finds consolation for her
strict vegetarian principles by stuffing herself full of candied fruit
and imposing an even more meatless diet on her long-suffering
husband, and this defeat reflects the perpetual triumph, in Huxley's
fictional world, of the heaviness of the flesh and the power of
misapplied idealism. For Martha Claxton loves both her husband and
her food with 'a heavy and menacing passion'; and the enthusiasm
which she has for 'spirituality and Jesus and *ahimsa* and beauty' is,
as the story makes clear, just an excuse for spiritual bullying.

The Claxtons is also characteristic of another feature of the books
Huxley published in the late twenties and early thirties: the dichotomy between his official view of the world – humanistic, rational,
sceptical – and the instinctive, almost unremitting pessimism implicit
in his imaginative writings. Thus, on the surface, he not only
recognizes Martha Claxton for what she is, but he also sees how
absurd Herbert Claxton is when he carries, even on his rare visits to
London, 'a rucksack overflowing with the leeks and cabbages needed
in such profusion to support a purely graminivorous family'. Yet he
cannot bring himself to follow out the implications of his ideas and
write a convincing story in which the Claxtons are defeated, and the
description of how a child's native intelligence is defeated by the
sheer weight and energy of certain adults is not new in his work. It
had already provided the plot, six years before *The Claxtons*, of the
better-known story, *Young Archimedes*, in 1924. There, a young
Italian boy Guido has an extraordinary talent for music and mathematics which is fostered by the narrator, an English writer who
lives more or less permanently abroad with his wife and small son.
But Guido comes from a poor family, and has a delicate, sensitive
beauty which attracts all the boundless but frustrated maternal
passion of *la signora* Bondi, the narrator's landlady. She so bullies
Guido's parents that they finally allow her to adopt him. She takes
him to live with her in Milan, where he dies of loneliness and a
broken heart, his musical talent stifled by her desire to show him off
as an infant prodigy. And it is again significant that the sensible,
intelligent, perceptive narrator – obviously, from his character,
family circumstances and mode of life, Huxley himself – can see
what is going to happen but is quite powerless to intervene.[16]

The less well-known, but nevertheless basically similar *Farcical History of Richard Greenow* appeared in what was in fact the first work of fiction that Huxley published, a collection of six short stories and a play entitled *Limbo* which appeared in January 1920. Richard Greenow, while an undergraduate at Canteloup College, Oxford, discovers one evening, while looking at some sentimental pictures, that he can go into a trance which enables him to fulfil every poverty-stricken intellectual's dream: churning out lucrative romantic fiction. He begins by detaching this side of his personality from his official, academic, highly intellectual self, and publishes under the name of Pearl Bellairs. But this other half of what he comes to realize is a fundamentally hermaphroditic personality refuses to be kept in its place. Conscious transvestism, initially a device to help him write better, becomes an irresistible temptation, and Richard Greenow ends his days in a lunatic asylum. The spirit, represented by his interest in ideas and mathematics, is again overwhelmed by the flesh, this time in the form of the heavy, clinging, inanely patriotic sentimentality of Pearl Bellairs, and in this respect the story constitutes a fitting opening to Huxley's career as a writer of fiction. But the story also underlines an essential factor in the making of all good-bad books, whether sentimental or pornographic, and it is a pleasant change to catch Huxley putting forward a brilliant generalization without quite realizing what he is doing. Only those who personally share the fantasies depicted in them can write either the books which sell in Soho or those which flaunt their sales on railway station bookstalls; and any intellectual who tries to follow Richard Greenow's example will run the risk of unleashing the sorcerer's apprentice lurking in his own subconscious mind.

From a purely literary point of view, the most successful presentation of this defeat of the spirit by the flesh lies in the two extracts from the Chronicles of Chrome which Henry Wimbush reads to his house guests in Huxley's first novel *Crome Yellow*, published in 1921. The first tells the story of Sir Hercules Lapith, a delicately formed aristocrat destined to grow to the height of only three feet four inches. He has the good fortune and persistence to create a private world where everything is kept down to his own size and from which what one of his poems describes as the 'huge mounds of matter', the 'gross and repulsive', 'giant ugliness' of ordinary men is excluded – everything, that is, except his own children. For his son Ferdinando grows into an enormous, over-size bully, who wreaks such havoc in Sir Hercules's world that the only escape left to his father is death. Yet while the flesh here triumphs quite unequivocally over the spirit, the second of Huxley's anecdotes in *Crome Yellow* offers a more cheering vision of the healthy revenge which the body sometimes reserves for those who drive it too hard. Three young ladies, anxious to conform to the Romantic idea that maidens are too pale, ethereal and unhappy ever to eat food, nevertheless mysteriously avoid dying of starvation. When the secret hiding place in which they yield to nature by washing down chicken and ham with hock and claret is accidentally discovered, they have no choice but to marry and like it. Acceptance of reality is a virtue which Huxley praises with great vigour and eloquence in the essays of his middle period – *Do What You Will* (1929) – and his insistence on what he calls, in *Point Counter Point*, 'the regulating body' recurs in various forms throughout his work.[17] It is, however, an insistence which is never wholly convincing, largely because Huxley never quite overcomes the dichotomy between what his knowledge and common sense tell him about the body, and the less satisfying experience which he personally has of it. The discovery of Georgiana, Emmeline and Caroline Lapith drinking hock with their chicken and ham is almost the only example in Huxley's work where food is described with any degree of appreciation; and it is not wholly surprising that he should, from the mid-nineteen-thirties onwards, have become almost as exclusively graminivorous as Herbert Claxton himself.

Both the style and the subject matter of Huxley's first three novels thus express the conflict between spirit and matter that runs through all his work. On the one hand, there is the brilliance which, in *Crome Yellow*, Mr Scogan is made to attribute solely to the works of the imaginary Knockespotch. 'There are extraordinary adventures,' he declares, 'and still more extraordinary speculations. Intelligences and emotions, relieved of all the imbecile preoccupations of civilized life, move in intricate and subtle dances, crossing and recrossing, advancing, retracting, impinging. An immense erudition and an immense fancy go hand in hand.' There are the jokes, as when Mr Scogan also suggests that Anglican clergy should distinguish themselves from the rest of the population by wearing not only their collars but also all their other garments the wrong way round, or Mr Cardan, in *Those Barren Leaves*, defends Etruscan as 'the great dead language of the future' because its total uselessness makes it so ideal a basis for a gentleman's education. There is also the apt but unexpected use of scientific metaphors, as when Francis Chellifer, commenting on how perfectly style flows from his fountain pen, remarks that 'in every drachm of blue-black ink a thousand *mots justes* are implicit, like the future characteristics of a man in a piece of chromosome',[18] and Huxley is always intellectually in control of what his characters say. Yet while he can order language as he wishes, presenting a view of life whose very iconoclasm is an invitation to happiness, the events he describes are always pessimistic.

Sometimes, it is true, the events are funny, just as the satire in *The Claxtons* is funny. In *Crome Yellow*, the young and aspiring novelist Denis Stone decides to transform himself from a poetic dreamer into a man of action; and, making no progress in his efforts

to seduce the delectable Anne, has a telegram sent summoning him
urgently back to London. It arrives just as Anne suddenly begins to
hint that she likes him, and this rather comic example of the mess in
which Huxley's heroes make of life when they have to leave the world
of ideas is paralleled by Theodore Gumbril's misadventures in *Antic
Hay*. His idyll with the girl whom he could really love is ruined
because he cannot resist the pleasure – which, fundamentally, he
despises – of lunching and being witty with Mrs Viveash; and when
a kindly old gentleman, a chance acquaintance on a train, offers to
give him a case of old brandy, Theodore has to leave before they can
exchange addresses. In *Those Barren Leaves*, however, the irony of
events is more tragic. Mr Cardan, who has no objections to marrying
a semi-idiot if this will save him from a penniless old age, removes
Grace Elver from the house where her brother is planning to murder
her for her money. But before the marriage can take place, she dies
of eating bad fish at an Italian lake-side inn, and Mr Cardan has
merely done Philip Elver's dirty work for him. As he sits in church
waiting for the funeral to begin, his reflections sum up the horror
which, for all its wit and sophistication, lies behind all Huxley's
work.

> But the greatest tragedy of the spirit is that sooner or later it
> succumbs to the flesh. Sooner or later every soul is stifled by the
> sick body; sooner or later there are no more thoughts, but only
> pain and vomiting and stupor. The tragedies of the spirit are mere
> struttings and posturings on the margin of life, and the spirit itself
> only an accidental exuberance, the product of spare vital energy,
> like the feathers on the head of a hoopoe or the innumerable
> populations of useless and foredoomed spermatozoa. . . . The farce
> is hideous, thought Mr Cardan, and in the worst possible taste.[19]

In *Antic Hay*, Mrs Viveash walks a knife-edge between invisible
gulfs of nihilism and despair, and proclaims in anticipation of
Samuel Beckett that 'Tomorrow will be as awful as to-day'.[20] But
she had lost her lover in the war, and her suffering had at least an
explicable origin in human greed, idiocy and violence. The initial
accident which prevented Grace Elver from growing up, like the
biological catastrophe which hastened her inevitable decay, are
inscribed in the inevitable processes of the natural world, and neither
art, science, religion nor philosophy can do anything about it.
Huxley's scientists, in particular, are unable to make any sensible
use of their knowledge, and the biologist Shearwater, in *Antic Hay*,
is only the first of a series of brilliant researchers who are fools
outside the laboratory. Cuckolded by Gumbril and Coleman, ridi-
culed by Mrs Viveash, he ends the novel pedalling madly on a
motionless bicycle, his perspiration gathered in a rubber bag as his

experiments with human physiology lead him into yet more meaningless behaviour. Yet although art can do as little as science to
improve the quality of human life, it is nevertheless the perfection
that can be glimpsed through certain artistic achievements which
provides one of the two values which Huxley allows to remain
relatively untouched in his first three novels.

Thus, in *Antic Hay*, Gumbril Senior has made a full-scale model
of the London which Sir Christopher Wren would have created had
his plans for rebuilding the city after the Great Fire been accepted.
It is a masterpiece of reason and elegance, with 'open spaces, broad
streets, sunlight, air, cleanliness, beauty, order and grandeur', and
the contrast between this ideal plan and the real but sordid city in
which the action takes place provides the central image for the
whole book. For Gumbril Senior, men failed to adopt Wren's plan
because 'they preferred ugliness and pettiness and dirt; they preferred the wretched human scale, the scale of the sickly body, not
of the mind', and he here seems to be speaking for Huxley himself
in laying insistence, as a good neo-Victorian should, upon the failure
of character which this deliberate choice implied. Yet although
people may be wrong to prefer, as they do in the post-war London
of *Antic Hay*, the 'melancholy and drawling song' played by 'grinning blackamoors' in a night-club to the 'pure, clear, unaffected'
happiness of the Mozart G minor quartet, their very possession
of a body seems to make this abandonment of purity almost inevitable.[21] The ideal exists in Huxley's first two novels almost as it exists
in the poetry of the Mallarmé whom he translated and so admired:
as something perpetually out of reach, and whose very perfection is
an added torment. Only at the end of *Antic Hay*, when Gumbril
Senior sells his Wren model in order to help a friend, does a human
being act in a way whose generosity equals the nobility suggested
by certain works of art. But the optimism about the human condition
which might be inferred from this particular action vanishes when
we learn why the scholar Porteous, Gumbril Senior's friend, needs so
much money. He has to pay the debts incurred by his only son, a
vapid wastrel whom Mrs Viveash and Gumbril junior have earlier
encountered gloomily wasting his substance in a night-club, declaim-
ing as he does so against the futility of a life devoted to pleasure.
Once again, matter defeats the spirit, loutish sons despoil their
kindly fathers, and brutish stupidity overcomes the human urge to
elegance and order.

For the reader acquainted with Huxley's later development, the
second solution proposed for the dilemmas explored in his early
fiction inevitably seems like a false start. Calamy, in *Those Barren
Leaves*, exchanges both the futile life of the country house party at
Mrs Aldwinkle's and the more constructive pleasures of literary
creation for a hermit's hut in the Apennines. Sir Isaac Newton, he

observes, 'practically abandoned mathematics for mysticism before he was thirty' and Huxley clearly intends the reader to see Calamy as representing the best way of seeking freedom from the heaviness of the flesh and the tyranny of the senses. Like Huxley's later mystical heroes, Calamy is interested not in a hypothetical life to come but in the life that we live here and now. In a world from which all traditional values have disappeared, and where the progress of science seems likely to produce, in Calamy's own words, 'a planet-wide race of Babbitts', his seems to be the only solution capable of liberating man.[22] What is curious is that Huxley should, after the publication of *Those Barren Leaves*, have postponed for over ten years any further exploration of what was to be his most important contribution to the twentieth-century debate between science and religion.

3 Humanism and contradiction

The publication, within the space of five years, of three novels, three volumes of short stories (*Limbo* in 1920, *Mortal Coils* in 1922, *Little Mexican* in 1924), two volumes of essays (*On the Margin* in 1923, *Along the Road* in 1925), together with a considerable amount of literary journalism, had freed Huxley from the financial worries of his early married life to the point where he was able, in September 1925, to embark on a trip round the world. 'To me,' he wrote in *Along the Road*, 'travelling is a vice, as hard to resist as the temptation to read promiscuously, omnivorously and without purpose', and in an essay entitled *Books for the Journey* he confirmed a legend which had already grown up about how he yielded to both temptations at once. The one book he always had with him, he wrote, was a volume of 'the twelfth, half-size edition of the *Encyclopedia Britannica*'. 'A stray volume,' he added, 'is like the mind of a learned madman; stored with correct ideas between which, however, there is no other connection than the fact that there is a B in both', and Bertrand Russell is even reputed to have said that you could always tell from Huxley's own conversation which particular volume of the *Encyclopedia Britannica* he had just been devouring.[1] It was certainly easier for the Huxleys to have a special packing case built for their copy of the *Encyclopedia Britannica* than to take their five-year-old son Matthew with them, and he was left to spend eight months or so with relatives.[2]

Almost half of *Jesting Pilate*, the book describing this round-the-world trip, was devoted to Huxley's experiences in India, and it was certainly the impact of Indian religion which turned him away from the mysticism presented so favourably at the end of *Those Barren Leaves*. 'One is all for religion,' he wrote, 'until one visits a really religious country. Then, one is all for drains, machinery and the minimum wage', and his attack on the social effects of religion in India is devastating. The worshippers who gather at Benares, intoning their prayers to prevent the sun from being eaten by a serpent during the eclipse, behave more stupidly than the animals themselves. Like the sacred bull who with one lick of its tongue removes all the rice which a morning's charity has deposited in a beggar's bowl, animals at least have the ability to do 'efficiently and by instinct the right, appropriate thing at the right moment – look for water when they feel thirst, make love in the mating season, rest or play when they have leisure.' Unlike men, they are not alienated by their own minds. They do not allow their intelligence and imagination to run away with them; and they never contradict, in favour of an absurd and unverifiable hypothesis, the instinctive wisdom of the body.

Neither the priests, doctrines nor practices of Hinduism move Huxley to anything but scorn. The first are represented not by one of what he ironically refers to as those 'pure-souled Oriental mystics who, we are told, are to leaven the materialism of our Western civilization', but by a fat, self-satisfied, and smelly old man; while the second are nothing but a means of tricking people into accepting an unbearable reality. 'Metempsychosis had to be invented, and the doctrine of *karma* elaborated with a frightful logic, before the serried, innumerable miseries of India could be satisfactorily accounted for', writes Huxley as his ship leaves India for Burma, and his agnosticism is here once again inseparable from his awareness of physical suffering. As for the third aspect of Hindu religion, the techniques of meditation which the later Huxley did so much to popularize in the West, these are dismissed as a 'mystic squint' which merely showed that 'the Lord Krishna knew all that there is to know about the art of self-hypnotism.'[3]

It is of course true, as the title of his book suggests, that Huxley will have little favourable to say about any of the countries he visits. So long as he remembers India, Henry Ford seems to him a greater man than the Buddha. But once he is in America, he realizes that the industrial civilization of the West, 'which is the creation of perhaps a hundred men of genius, assisted by a few thousand intelligent and industrious disciples, exists for the millions, whose minds are indistinguishable in quality from those of the average humans of the paleolithic age'; and at times, he too is so depressed as to be tempted by metaphysics. The 'real' Japan, which he sees in the industrial suburbs of Kyoto, strikes him as 'so repulsive that we are compelled, if we have any pride in our country or our human species, to practise a wholesale Christian Science on it and deny it reality.' Some beliefs, however, do survive at the end of *Jesting Pilate*. The first, the conviction that 'it takes all sorts to make a world' and consequently that 'the completest possible tolerance' should be extended to all activities except those which stultify 'the fundamental values', is easy to understand. The others are more vaguely defined as 'the established spiritual values' and since Huxley has already said that there is no hope for India until 'the Hindus and the Moslems are as tepidly enthusiastic about their religion as we are about the Church of England', it is difficult to see quite what he means. A more definite article of faith is a passionate acceptance of our own world as something real, valuable 'wide, incredibly varied and more fantastic than any product of the imagination', and this is certainly not a belief remarkable for its spirituality.[4] Moreover, by the time *Jesting Pilate* was published in October 1926, Huxley had renewed his acquaintanceship with D. H. Lawrence; and it was this writer's

C

'great religion' of 'a belief in the blood, the flesh, as being wiser than the intellect' which was to lead Huxley even further from the mysticism apparently advocated by the ending of *Those Barren Leaves*.

Huxley had first met Lawrence in 1915, at the suggestion of Lady Ottoline Morrell. They liked each other immediately, with Huxley agreeing to join the colony which Lawrence was then hoping to found in Florida, while Lawrence wrote to Lady Ottoline that he 'liked Huxley *very* much', but this first meeting yielded no permanent results. After 1919, Lawrence visited England rarely and the two men drifted apart until after Huxley's return from his round-the-world trip in June 1926. Their friendship then moved on to a firmer and more permanent footing, with Maria Huxley typing out the manuscript of *Lady Chatterley's Lover* for an Italian printer – and having to be discouraged by Lawrence himself from introducing some of his four-letter words into her conversation – and Lawrence becoming a frequent visitor to the various houses which the Huxleys rented in France and Italy. Initially, it seems, there were some areas of purely intellectual disagreement. Huxley was amazed that so intelligent a man could really believe that the moon was 'a globe of dynamic substance, like radium or phosphorus, coagulated upon a vivid pole of energy', and could not understand Lawrence going against all the evidence in favour of the theory of evolution because he 'did not feel it there: in the solar plexus'.[5] After a little time, however, Huxley realized the futility of wasting his time arguing with a man who had so much to offer, and preferred to listen. And it was from Lawrence that he absorbed the assertive, defiantly anti-religious and enthusiastically sensual humanism which provided a central theme for the two major works of his second, middle period: the novel, *Point Counter Point*, published in October 1928; and the collection of essays, *Do What You Will* published in 1929. Their violent attack on Baudelaire, Pascal, Swift and Wordsworth provides an obvious commentary on the argument in the novel, while at the same time the admiration they express for Blake, D. H. Lawrence and Robert Burns constitutes a brief high-water mark both in Huxley's optimism about human nature and in his agnosticism.

Huxley's first three novels had all been to some extent *romans à clef*. In *Crome Yellow*, Lady Ottoline Morrell had at least partly inspired the creation of Priscilla Wimbush, Denis Stone was clearly Huxley himself, while Mr Scogan, with his 'small, saurian hand' and indefatigable voice, was a mixture of Bertrand Russell and the Norman Douglas of *South Wind*. Similarly, in *Antic Hay*, Shearwater was considered by some to be a satirical portrait of J. B. S. Haldane, both the conversation and the jokes of Coleman were known to be based on the behaviour of Philip Heseltine, while no less a figure than Wyndham Lewis had apparently provided the model for the painter Lypiatt.[6] Indeed, so numerous were the other, less easily identifiable portraits, that the success of Huxley's first three novels was attributed by some people to a prurient curiosity about the bohemian goings-on in London café society. In addition to being a more complex and ambitious literary undertaking than his early novels, *Point Counter Point* also contained more characters than either *Antic Hay* or *Those Barren Leaves*, and it was even easier to give some of them their 'real' names. In particular, it offered in Mark Rampion a figure whom everyone but Lawrence himself, who described him as a 'dreadful windbag', recognized as an expression of his own ideas and personality, and who is the only person in any novel of Huxley's early or middle period whose view of life is presented with complete sympathy. In particular, Rampion's attacks on industrialism, his contemptuous dismissal of Calvin, Knox, Baxter and Wesley as 'revolting monsters',[7] his strictures on all those, whether they be Jesus, Ford or Newton, who seek to turn man's attention away from the immediate realities of physical existence, all provide a standard whereby the other characters in the novel are found wanting. Rampion is also the only person in Huxley's non-mystical fiction who makes his ideas and conduct coincide, and in this sense is the hero of the novel. Neither is this favourable presentation of Lawrence's philosophy and personality the only sign of his influence on Huxley's way of thinking. In *Point Counter Point*, Philip Quarles is obviously Huxley himself, and Quarles is an enthusiastic supporter of Rampion's ideas. However, unlike the Huxley of *Do What You Will*, he rightly suspects that he is 'congenitally incapable of living wholly and harmoniously',[8] and *Point Counter Point* is a more accurate guide than the aggressively agnostic essays of how Huxley continued to see the world in the late nineteen-twenties.

In Huxley's first three novels, the ideas often had little relationship either with the plot or with the way in which the events were presented to the reader. His literary models at that time, as J. S. Fraser has observed, were not only the Peacock of *Crotchet Castle* or *Nightmare Abbey*, but also Ronald Firbank and the Norman Douglas of *South Wind*; and in all these novels we do indeed have, in both plot and atmosphere, 'the impact of relaxed mediterranean models on Anglo-Saxon respectability'. In *Point Counter Point*, the action takes place in England, and the characters are more fully integrated into the society in which they live. Several are seen against the background of their marriages, their social position or their professional activity, and Huxley modestly admitted to Laura Archera in the late 1950s that the novel was 'thought to be important as a picture of English society at that time'.[9] In this respect, of course, some aspects inevitably have a somewhat dated air. Lucy Tantamount, perhaps modelled as much on the Lady Griffiths of André Gide's *Les Faux-Monnayeurs* as on the actual person whose name is still left tantalizingly blank in one of D. H. Lawrence's letters about *Point Counter Point*, is very much the vamp of the nineteen-twenties tradition, and her remark that life would have some point if it were 'always like dancing with a professional' situates the action very firmly in the disillusioned world of *thé-dansant* and the tango. Similarly, when Walter Bidlake's inability to ask Burlap for more money is presented as meaning that 'poor Marjorie would have to go without new clothes and a second maid', the whole atmosphere moves into a different and even slightly idyllic world.[10]

The influence of Gide's *Les Faux-Monnayeurs*, published in 1926, may also be detectable in two other aspects of *Point Counter Point*: Huxley's decision to put the novelist Philip Quarles in the novel, making him keep a notebook in which he comments on the problems of novel-writing; and the greater importance which he obviously wishes his readers to attach to the way in which the story is told. Indeed, Huxley draws attention to the importance of technique by the ideas which Philip Quarles expresses in his diary on the 'musicalization of fiction'. 'Not in the symbolist way,' Quarles explains, 'by subordinating sense to sound . . . but on a large scale, in the constructions', and he goes on to speak of how one can modulate 'not merely from one key to another but from mood to mood'. The plot of *Point Counter Point* can indeed be seen in a number of different, complementary ways which are also linked together by Huxley's own temperament and obsessions. It can be seen as arranged round three deaths: that of little Phil, Philip Quarles's son, from meningitis; that of John Bidlake, his father-in-law, from cancer; and that of Everard Webley, who almost becomes Elinor Quarles's lover but who is murdered by Spandrell and Illidge. Alternatively – or, perhaps, in addition, since all three deaths are associated with one another through the character of Philip Quarles – it can be seen as a study of family relationships, similarities and contrasts. John Bidlake's younger son has died of cancer, so that there is a kind of inverted hereditary relationship about the disease which is now killing him; Philip and Elinor Quarles are both children of unhappy marriages, and seem in danger of repeating their parents' problems in a different form; while Walter Bidlake and his sister Elinor are weak, sentimental people, who are both attracted in their sexual life by strong characters such as Lucy Tantamount and Everard Webley. The failure of Walter's affair with Marjorie Carling, like the difficulties in Philip Quarles's marriage to Elinor, also bring out by contrast the importance of the successful partnership between Mark and Mary Rampion, so that Huxley's consciously adopted technique of narration seems to express his admiration for Lawrence's personality and ideas.

There is also a temporal relationship between the different events.

At the same time that the foetus grows in Marjorie Carling's uterus, transforming her initial misery into the physical euphoria and spiritual peace of the third and fourth months of pregnancy, the cancer proliferating in John Bidlake's pylorus changes the delight which he had found in eating, drinking and making love into the fury of a trapped animal in a world where, as Elinor Quarles comes to realize, 'the very possession of a body is a cynical comment on the soul and all its ways'.[11] The novel begins with Walter Bidlake – like Philip Quarles, the idealistic and fastidious son of a sexually promiscuous father – guiltily trying to escape from the consequences of seducing Marjorie Carling, and the events of her pregnancy run parallel to the scandal caused in the Quarles family by the revelation that one of Mr Quarles senior's mistresses is going to have a baby. The novel also describes several other adulterous affairs before ending with the imminent seduction of Beatrice Gilray by Walter Burlap, and the sexual behaviour of the characters is almost uniformly bad. The optimistic, 'life-worshipping' Huxley of *Do What You Will* might well imply, by his regret that Baudelaire's path was not 'strewn with seduced young girls, adulterous wives, and flagellated actresses' that the sins of the flesh are really rather jolly. But the novelist who analyses the miseries of illicit sex is far less convinced of its pagan charms, and the dichotomy already visible in Huxley's first three novels between intellectual liberation and enslavement to the flesh recurs in a different form. In *Point Counter Point*, human beings are depicted as incapable on moral and sexual grounds of living according to the precepts of *Do What You Will*, and the path consequently lies wide open to the mysticism of *Eyeless in Gaza* and *Ends and Means*.

The essentially optimistic humanism of *Do What You Will* has indeed very little effect on the vision of reality presented in the novel which seems at first sight to illustrate the findings of the essays. Just as the Wren model, in *Antic Hay*, underlined the sordidness of post-war London and represented an ideal which could never be attained in actual experience, so the Bach fugue in the first chapter of *Point Counter Point* emphasizes by contrast how stupidly people are behaving at the elegant reception where it is played. The only deliberately planned series of events in *Point Counter Point* leads from Maurice Spandrell's calculated murder of Everard Webley to his own more philosophically conceived suicide; and as Webley's men avenge their leader's death, the 'counterpoint of serenities' in Beethoven's *heilige Dankgesang* presents a 'miraculous paradox of eternal life and eternal repose' whose principal role is again to bring out by contrast the futility of what human beings actually do. For all Huxley's attempt to present Rampion as the hero and to depict his way of life as a viable ideal, both the events in the novel and the relationship between them lead to the same conclusion: life is a meaningless joke, in which the marvel of Everard Webley's suddenly realized love for Elinor is immediately followed by his murder, and the serenely beautiful evening light in which she drives home is a prelude to the death in agony of her only son. When D. H. Lawrence dismissed the character of Mark Rampion as a 'windbag', he was not only exhibiting his well-known tendency to reject as invalid anybody else's formulation of his own ideas. He was also making a justified criticism of Huxley's failure, in *Point Counter Point*, to bring his imaginative vision of reality into line with the 'religion of life-worship' which he now officially espoused.

This failure is not, of course, something of which the Huxley who wrote *Point Counter Point* was unaware. He is clearly talking about himself when he makes Philip Quarles acknowledge, in his diary, that his own 'continued and excessive indulgence in the vices of informative reading and abstract generalization' marked a congenital inability to live 'wholly and harmoniously', and he also gives Philip Quarles a physical handicap comparable to his own in order to help explain why his hero experiences such difficulty in living life to the full. As a result of a childhood accident, Philip Quarles is lame in one leg, and has to wear a heavy, surgical boot. For Rachel Quarles, his mother, this lameness prevented Philip from mixing fully with his equals during the crucial period of his adolescence, and thus predestined him to the solitary life of books and abstract ideas. '*Keratitis punctata*', wrote Huxley in 1933, in a letter to Naomi Mitchison, 'shaped and continues to shape me'[12] and he is clearly translating his own personal experience into this aspect of *Point Counter Point*. What he does not mention, for to do so might have spoilt the slightly romantic, Thomas Mannish creation of Philip Quarles, was that he himself had another physical characteristic which increased his feeling of separation from the rest of mankind: his height. He stood six foot four, and small boys would occasionally inquire, as he walked through the London streets, 'Cold up there, guv'nor?' Neither his physique, social position, past experience nor creative imagination fitted Huxley for the role of life-worshipper which he assumed in the late nineteen-twenties, and his brilliant diagnosis of his inability to 'live wholly and harmoniously' makes *Point Counter Point* not only a far more perceptive book than *Do What You Will* but also a more honest one.

D. H. Lawrence also recognized, however, an aspect of Huxley's character which is not attributed to the Philip Quarles of *Point Counter Point*: an almost pathological obsession with physical suffering and acts of physical violence. 'If you can only palpitate to murder, suicide and rape, in their various degrees, and you state plainly that this is so – *caro*, however are we to live through the days?' wrote Lawrence in a letter to Huxley in 1929, and continued: 'It is as you say – intellectual appreciation does not amount to so much, it's what you thrill to. And if murder, suicide, rape is what you thrill to, and nothing else, then it's your destiny – you can't change it *mentally*.'[13] Huxley was, in fact, a man of extraordinary contradictions as well as outstanding intellect: an apostle of toleration who wrote of 'grinning blackamoors' and 'repulsive German Jews' in terms that make the modern reader wince; an immensely gentle, kind and considerate man, whose novels are full of murders, abortions, whippings, torments, amputations, betrayals, maimings and descriptions of organized oppression; an inheritor of the austerest traditions of scientific integrity who showed the most amazing credulity with regard to unorthodox medicine; a puritanical, neo-Victorian intellectual whose experiments with mescalin helped to spark off the Californian drug culture of the nineteen-sixties. The discrepancy between *Do What You Will* and *Point Counter Point* is the first important example of how openly these contradictions showed themselves, as well as the most convincing explanation of why it was not long before he reverted to mysticism.

The persistently gloomy note of Huxley's fiction has also led critics to make attacks on him which seem inspired more by moral or political disapproval than by a sympathetic reading of his work. In 1936, in *The Coming Struggle for Power*, John Strachey wrote: 'His findings are always the same. Go where you like, "Do What You Will", you will never escape from the smell of ordure and decay', while John McCormick, in 1957, went even further than the immediate evidence justified when he declared, in a study of the later novels, that 'Huxley's own inability to love' had 'turned into a hatred of women and humanity'.[14] It is certainly because of the contradiction which Lawrence noted between Huxley's niceness as a person and the 'precocious adolescent' who 'palpitated only to murder, suicide and rape' that *Point Counter Point*, in so far as it is meant as an illustration of the ideas put forward in *Do What You Will*, is so obvious a failure. The writers whom Huxley attacks most eloquently in his essays – Pascal and Baudelaire – are the very ones whose ideas are vindicated by what happens in the novel, for when Philip Quarles gives up what he had earlier regarded as 'the highest of human tasks' because of his realization that 'this famous Search for Truth is just an amusement, a distraction like any other', he might almost be paraphrasing Pascal's view that even the act of writing apologia for the Christian religion is merely another form of escaping from reality through *le divertissement*.[15] Baudelaire, too, is equally present both in the plot of the novel and in the description of Lucy Tantamount making love. She does so with an expression of 'grave and attentive suffering' on her face, 'as though the agonizing pleasure were a profound and difficult experience to be grasped only by intense concentration', and Huxley's sentence is a virtual if perhaps unconscious paraphrase of Baudelaire's remark that the act

of love has 'a strong similarity to torture or to a surgical operation'.[16] What is even more significant, however, is that the character
who is obviously based upon Baudelaire, the life-hater Spandrell,
plays a far more active and influential role in the plot of the book
than either its ostensible hero, Mark Rampion, or the character
representing Huxley himself. Thus it is Spandrell who murders
Everard Webley, and who is, moreover, inspired to do so by motives
which are fully comprehensible only in terms of the Freudianism
which both Huxley and Lawrence officially rejected. Madame
Baudelaire's remarriage, when her son was seven, to the dashing
and authoritarian Major Aupick is translated in *Point Counter Point*
into the remarriage of Maurice Spandrell's mother, when her son is
fifteen, to Major Knoyle, and in both cases the jealousy which the
sons feel towards their stepfathers takes a political turn. Baudelaire,
it is alleged, manned the barricades during the 1848 revolution with
the cry of 'Il faut fusiller le Général Aupick'. Spandrell goes one
better by actually succeeding in his plot to kill Everard Webley, the
leader of the British Freemen, and it is interesting to contrast
Huxley's intellectual and intuitive grasp of political matters with his
apparent inability to see how completely the events in *Point Counter
Point* invalidated the argument put forward in *Do What You Will*.
In 1928, when *Point Counter Point* was published, Oswald Mosley
was still a member of the Labour Party, and even enjoyed something
of a reputation as a liberal. As late as February 1929, D. H. Lawrence
himself was suggesting that Sir Oswald Mosley 'the socialist M.P.'
might ask a question in the House about the confiscation by the
police of his book *Pansies*, and the obviously Fascist inspiration, in
Point Counter Point, of Webley and his Green Shirts anticipates a
development in both Mosley's own career and in English politics
generally which did not take place until several years later.[17]

Neither is Spandrell the only character in *Point Counter Point* who
is based upon a real person of whose attitudes and behaviour Huxley
disapproved, yet who is more successful than Mark Rampion in
influencing other people's lives. Burlap, a caricature of Middleton
Murray, has an overwhelming effect on at least two people – Beatrice
Gilray, who becomes his mistress, and Ethel Cobbet, whom he
drives to suicide – and triumphs at the end of the novel in a scene
which epitomizes both Huxley's comic vision and his appreciation
of the contribution which neo-Freudian psychology could make to
the novel.

> That night he and Beatrice pretended to be little children and had
> their bath together. Two little children sitting at opposite ends of
> the big old-fashioned bath. And what a romp they had! The bath-
> room was drenched with their splashings. Of such is the Kingdom
> of Heaven.

Yet even Burlap can make mistakes, and, like Emma Bovary thinking that she was predestined to be a great romantic heroine – or, one may add, Aldous Huxley thinking he could be a Lawrentian life-worshipper – can be misled by his own imagination. From the verses she submitted to the *Literary World*, he had imagined Romola Saville to be the very incarnation of experienced but vulnerable passion. The name turns out to be the pseudonym for two elderly, ugly Lesbians, and Burlap's failure to appreciate the difference between literature and reality echoes in a comical vein the mistake which Walter Bidlake makes elsewhere in the novel when he tries to base his affair with Marjorie Carling on the poetry of Shelley; or the one which Miss Fulkes, little Phil's governess, makes when she imagines that we must needs love the noblest when we see it but vastly prefers *The Mystery of the Castlemaine Emeralds* to Adam Smith's *The Wealth of Nations*.

Nowhere, however, is this theme of self-deception more effectively used than in Huxley's depiction of Illidge, Lord Tantamount's research assistant, and the one major character in his novels not to be a member by birth of the upper middle-class. Illidge is a scholarship boy from the slums of Rochdale, passionately devoted both to science and to the cause of violent revolution, and his very first appearance introduces this theme of the difference between how people appear in their own eyes and what they are like for other people. Deeply conscious, in the presence of Lady Tantamount's elegant guests, of how shabby he looks in his blue serge suit, Illidge imagines himself as a visitor from another planet, scornfully condescending to visit the world of lower mortals. Unfortunately, 'too busy being a Martian to look where he is going', he slips and almost falls, and his discomfiture in this opening scene is echoed in a more serious and tragic vein at the end of the novel. Theoretically, Illidge is all for murder if it serves the cause of the revolution. As a scientist, he is also wholly free of the moral scruples which might affect lesser mortals. Yet when Spandrell takes him up on his boast and makes him help in the murder of Webley, Illidge discovers how 'utterly irrelevant' all his scientific principles and all his resentment against society are to 'the fact of these stiffening limbs, this mouth that gaped, these half-shut, glazed and secretly staring eyes'. Just as he continues to support his mother when he knows, as Spandrell says, that 'in any properly organized society, she'd be put into the lethal chamber', Illidge is totally unable to bring his emotional reactions to experience into line with his scientific and political convictions. In his case, the possession of a soul is more 'an ironic comment on the body and all its ways', and his horror at what he and Spandrell have done underlines the seriousness of the major philosophical problem lying behind Huxley's novels. In the context of the Darwinism so brilliantly defended by Thomas Henry Huxley, man is simply a product of the wholly amoral and fundamentally accidental process which governs the evolution of all forms of life. The scientific determinism so ardently espoused by Illidge is the logical consequence of the vision of reality produced by this and other aspects of nineteenth-century science, and his view of the world, though already old-fashioned in 1928,[18] was nevertheless still consistent with the evidence available. But none of the characters in Huxley's novels can accept the status of biological sports given to them by this scientific philosophy which they either hope or fear may be true. Both the grief which Elinor Quarles feels at the death of her son and the guilt which assails Illidge at the death of his enemy are symptoms of the contradiction which runs through all Huxley's work: man is an animal, and as such is subject to the mindless laws and irrational whims of the biological universe; but he cannot bring his ideas into line with this reality, and is tormented by feelings which would be meaningful only if there were a God who 'knew the fall of the sparrow' (Matthew x, 29), who had really ordained that man should not kill, and who would 'bring all things to judgment'.

In 1964 Jean-Paul Sartre expressed very much the same idea as Huxley when he described human beings as '*des animaux sinistrés*' (animals struck with disaster),[19] and Huxley's anticipation of what is perhaps the major theme of atheistic existentialism also inspires some of the best passages of intellectual and evocative writing in *Point Counter Point*. The ability to see human events in scientific terms, which Huxley exploited for semi-comic effect both in the *Fifth Philosopher's Song* and in the joke about the stylistic potentialities of Calamy's ink, takes on a deeper and more disturbing tone in the two descriptions, one wholly serious, the other potentially comic, of Marjorie Carling's pregnancy.

Six months from now her baby would be born. Something that had been a single cell, a cluster of cells, a little sac of tissue, a kind of worm, a potential fish with gills, stirred in her womb and would one day become a man – a grown man, suffering and enjoying, loving and hating, thinking, remembering, imagining. And what had been a blob of jelly within her body would invent a god and worship; what had been a kind of fish would create and, having created, would become the battle-ground of disputing good and evil; what had blindly lived in her as a parasitic worm would look at the stars, would listen to music, would read poetry.

A cell had multiplied itself and become a worm, the worm had become a fish, the fish was turning into the foetus of a mammal. Marjorie felt sick and tired. Fifteen years hence a boy would be confirmed. Enormous in his robes, like a full-rigged ship, the

Bishop would say: 'Do ye here in the presence of God, and of this congregation, renew the solemn promise and vow that was made in your name at your Baptism?' And the ex-fish would answer with passionate conviction: 'I do.'[20]

The superiority of *Point Counter Point* over earlier novels lies in the greater impact which Huxley allows the moral issues raised by man's knowledge of his own complex nature to make on both himself and his readers. At the beginning of *Crome Yellow*, the two hours which Denis spends travelling to Crome are merely 'the two hours in which he might have done so much – written the perfect poem, for example, or read the one illuminating book'. In *Point Counter Point*, as Illidge sits waiting for the darkness which will enable him and Spandrell to hide Everard Webley's body, the two hours which can be grasped intellectually as giving time enough to 'listen to the Ninth Symphony and a couple of the posthumous quartets, to transfer a luncheon from the stomach to the small intestine, to read *Macbeth*, to die of snake bite or earn one-and-eight pence as a charwoman' seem unending.[21] Not only does man inhabit a world in which, as Calamy realized, no single account of reality can ever hope to be correct. The subjective, existential awareness which he has of his own fate cannot be reconciled with his intellectual understanding of the world.

In one of his very first stories, *Happily ever After* (1920), Huxley is clearly describing himself when he speaks of the main character, Guy Lambourne, as being 'intellectually a Voltairean' but 'emotionally a Bunyanite'.[22] At the time of writing *Point Counter Point* and *Do What You Will* the Voltairean side of his nature was officially uppermost, and was being to some extent deliberately fostered by D. H. Lawrence. It was he who encouraged Huxley to write the book on 'the great perverts' which clearly became *Do What You Will*, and Huxley's essay on Pascal is in fact a restatement of Voltaire's attack. Like Voltaire, Huxley argues that Pascal is striving to make everybody as sick as he was, and maintains that to impose his own invalid's philosophy upon the whole range of human temperament is 'almost as unjustifiable as it is for a man to impose a human universe on a sea urchin'.[23] Against Pascal's asceticism and spiritual totalitarianism, Huxley argues that each man has 'as much right to his world view as he has to his kidneys', and the physiology which he uses so frequently to present a depressed and depressing picture of mankind is here used for its liberation. What is impressive about this essay, however, is less its relatively unoriginal content than its relation to the rest of Huxley's work. It shows, to begin with, a quite remarkable ability to step outside his own temperamental sympathy with Bunyanism and appreciate the force of the arguments for a non-Christian, non-ascetic philosophy. It is an ability that has always been strangely lacking in the Bunyans, the Pascals and the Baudelaires, and the fact that Huxley later changed his mind about Pascal, to the point of commenting in his essay on Maine de Biran, in 1953, on the shallowness and deliberately frivolous incomprehension of Voltaire's remarks on the *Pensées*, in no way affects the validity of the arguments that he put forward in 1929.[24] Just as the satirical account of Herbert Claxton's vegetarianism, or Philip Quarles's comment on the 'profound silliness of saintly people' cut the heroes of Huxley's own later novels down to size, so the statement in *Do What You Will* that 'mystical experiences happen because they do happen, because that is what the human mind is like' is fair comment on Huxley's mysticism. It is nevertheless in Huxley's own 'bovarystic angle', the contrast between what his vision of himself as a vigorous, god-baiting 'life-worshipper', and the real personality which reveals itself in *Point Counter Point*, that the reasons for his later adoption of mysticism can be found.

At least in theory, the satirical portraits in *Point Counter Point* of Burlap and Sidney Quarles, like the more complex and less hostile description of Illidge, imply a clear recommendation on how people should try to order their lives. Honesty about one's own personality and motives, the observance of Polonius's maxim of 'this above all: to thine own self be true', are the essential virtues, and it is fully consistent with the agnosticism of *Do What You Will* that man should base his life on the open-eyed acceptance of himself and the world as they really are. Yet there are, within the novel itself, a number of reasons why neither the attitude of the life-worshipper nor this ethic of personal honesty can provide an adequate basis for human existence. If reality is as appalling as the death of little Phil suggests, the vague but sincere religiosity with which Rachel Quarles accepts her own fate and helps other people to bear theirs becomes a major virtue; and if life is as cruel as the existence of meningitis seems to imply, there is no reason whatsoever to worship it. In his preface to the edition of Lawrence's letters which he published in 1932, Huxley described Lawrence's ideas as involving what he called 'the Doctrine of Cosmic Pointlessness', and it is somewhat paradoxical, to say the least, to use the word 'worship' in a context where neither goodness, beauty, purpose nor salvation are in any way relevant. Neither does the virtue of sincerity hold out very much promise to those who, like Huxley himself, are blessed or cursed with the ability to see every side of every question, and Huxley's self-portrait through the character of Philip Quarles constantly emphasizes why the philosophy of life-worship never became, for Huxley himself, anything more than an intellectual ideal. If one has what Huxley makes Philip Quarles describe as an amoeba-like intellect, 'capable of flowing in all directions, of engulfing every object in its path, of trickling into every crevice, of filling every mould and,

having engulfed, of flowing on towards other obstacles, other recep-
tacles, leaving the first empty and dry', then one cannot be faithful
to any central self.

The unflattering portrait which Huxley gives of himself in *Point
Counter Point* does not, of course, invalidate the criticism put
forward in *Do What You Will* of those thinkers who, like Pascal,
tried to force the whole of humanity into one particular mould.
Indeed, in so far as there is a Philip Quarles in each and every one
of us, Huxley's remark in his essay on Pascal that he prefers being
'dangerously free and alive to being safely mummified' represents
an attitude which he never really abandoned. There is also another
aspect of D. H. Lawrence's ideas which Huxley presents favourably
in *Point Counter Point* and to which he remained faithful throughout
his career as a writer and thinker.

> If men went about satisfying their instinctive desires only when
> they genuinely felt them, like the animals you're so contemptuous
> of', Rampion tells Spandrell, 'they'd behave a damned sight better
> than the majority of civilized human beings behave to-day. It isn't
> natural appetite and spontaneous instinctive desire that make men
> so beastly – no, "beastly" is the wrong word; it implies an insult
> to the animals – so all-too-humanly bad and vicious then. It's the
> imagination, it's the intellect, its principles, its tradition and
> education. Leave the instincts to themselves and they'll do very
> little mischief.'

Never, even at his most intensely mystical, did Huxley give up his
belief in what he called elsewhere the 'deep wisdom of the body',[25]
and this again, like the less permanent rejection of the mysticism
praised at the end of *Those Barren Leaves*, seems to have been something first instilled into him by his visit to India. Coming from
someone whose own body had played him so many tricks, and who
had commented so often on its unconscious and casual cruelties, this
suggestion of Huxley's that man might do better if he were to listen
more to his body and less to his mind, inevitably strikes a rather
peculiar note. It is none the less fully consistent both with the overwhelming impact which the suicide of his brother Trevenen had
upon him in 1914, and with the much less dramatic incident of the
bull at Benares in 1925. What is 'best and noble' in human beings,
their intellect and imagination, can lead them to kill themselves.
What is most typically animal, the instinctive drive to physical
survival, can never do harm.

It was nevertheless some time before Huxley returned to the theme
of how man ought best to order his life. Between the appearance of
Point Counter Point in 1928 and the publication of his next major
novel, *Eyeless in Gaza*, in 1936, there is something of a pause in the

almost frantic productivity that had characterized his work in the nineteen-twenties. In retrospect, it seems as though he were almost drawing breath before setting out on his 'second period', and husbanding his energies before embarking on the task of reconciling science and mysticism. This would not, however, be a wholly accurate account of Huxley's life between 1928 and 1936. The publication of *Point Counter Point* cast something of a shadow over his relationship with his wife, and D. H. Lawrence told Lady Ottoline Morrell in February 1929 how he thought that 'the *Counter-Point* book sort of got between them'. 'She minded *Point Counter Point*', he wrote later in the same month to E. W. Brewster, ' – his killing the child – it was all too life-like and horrible – . . . I think Maria hardly forgives it. And perhaps now he's sorry he did it.' The character of Philip Quarles was indeed so autobiographical that the death of little Phil inevitably takes on some curious personal overtones, while the dissection of Quarles's relationship with Elinor cannot have made Huxley's own marriage any easier. In a letter written in 1953 to his son Matthew, Huxley wrote both of his own inadequacy as a father and of the 'terrible dryness' that characterized certain years in his marriage. Another curious resemblance between Aldous Huxley and his grandfather lies in the fact that both should have had to rely heavily on their wives to make contact with the rest of the world and find out how ordinary people thought and felt.[26] *Point Counter Point* did nevertheless have some compensating advantages. As D. H. Lawrence somewhat tartly remarked, it enabled the Huxleys to buy a new car, a ten horsepower Citröen, in which Huxley could indulge his passion for high-speed travelling – Maria drove – on the then deserted Italian roads, and added to the very considerable financial independence that they now enjoyed. For all the strictures laid upon it by Wyndham Lewis, who analysed its opening page as exemplifying 'the very voice of "Fiction" as practised by the most characteristic of lady novelists',[27] *Point Counter Point* raised Huxley's general standing in the world of letters and showed that he was becoming more than an *enfant terrible* of the nineteen-twenties. Two of the books which he published in the eight years between *Point Counter Point* and *Eyeless in Gaza* strengthened the claim, ironically referred to in Somerset Maugham's *Cakes and Ale* in 1930, to be currently considered as 'England's leading novelist', and are unique in his work in having received almost unanimous praise from English literary critics.

The first of these was *The Letters of D. H. Lawrence*, a selection of the correspondence which he began collecting after Lawrence's death in 1930 and published in 1932. Whatever resentment Lawrence may have felt in seeing his ideas expounded by a 'gasbag' like Rampion, Huxley was one of the few friends with whom he maintained a stable relationship. Huxley helped to nurse Lawrence through his last illness and was with him when he died. F. R. Leavis, reviewing the *Letters* in *Scrutiny*, concluded by adding that 'we are all heavily in Mr. Aldous Huxley's debt' and that 'the index, so necessary, is almost perfect'; and Harry T. Moore, providing a fuller edition thirty years later, remarked that Huxley's collection, in its 'brilliant introduction and in its arrangement of the letters . . . prepared a background for the better understanding of Lawrence's work and of the man himself'.[28] Neither was Lawrence the only intellectual and literary mentor to whom Huxley paid tribute in 1932. On 4 May he delivered the Thomas Huxley Memorial lecture at Imperial College, choosing as his subject *T. H. Huxley as a Man of Letters*. His ability to analyse style, like the scholarship which he showed both in his edition of Lawrence's letters and in later historical works such as *Grey Eminence* or *The Devils of Loudun*, indicate what an admirable University teacher was lost when no Oxford college could be persuaded to make him a fellow in 1918. Nevertheless, there were compensations for his readers if not for the students taught by the nonentities doubtless appointed in his stead. His freedom to live and write as he chose helped to produce, in *Brave New World* (1932), perhaps the best piece of science fiction ever written, the most consistently up to date of all the books about the future which were then appearing, as P. G. Wodehouse wrote to Bill Townend, 'like a ruddy epidemic'.[29]

4 *Brave New World*

One of the many resemblances between Aldous Huxley and his grandfather lies in the interest which both men took in the question of human fertility. For Thomas Henry, it seems – rather surprisingly – to have been a personal problem as well as a concern natural in a biologist, for in 1858 he wrote to his friend Dr Dyster that he wished 'a revised version of the Genus Homo would come out, at any rate as far as the female part of it is concerned – one half of them seem to me doomed to incessant misery so long as they are capable of childbirth'.[1] Unlike T. H. Huxley, who eventually fathered six children, Aldous had only one son, and his concern with the problem was of a more general nature. It nevertheless recurs with obsessive force in almost all his books, and it is remarkable how early he appreciated the gravity of what is now mankind's gravest problem. In 1925 he was already commenting that any of his grandchildren who wanted to 'get away from it all' would have to take their holidays in Central Asia, and in 1956 he expressed the same idea in dramatically statistical terms when he wrote in an essay entitled *The Desert*, that 'solitude is receding at the rate of four and a half kilometres per annum'. Long before ecology, conservation and environmental studies had become fashionable concerns, he made Lord Edward Tantamount in *Point Counter Point*, speak of the 'natural, cosmic revolution' which would make man bankrupt if he continued to plunder the planet, and in *Do What You Will* he goes so far as to argue that mankind has already passed the point of no return. Since the productivity of the machine has permitted the creation of twice the number of people than can be supported by a return of the primitive agricultural methods advocated by Gandhi, the purest idealism could have the most disastrous consequences. Tamberlaine's butcheries would be 'insignificant indeed compared with the massacres so earnestly advocated by our mild and gramini-vorous Mahatma', and the combination between natural fertility and human ingenuity has sprung a trap more devilish than disease itself.[2]

It is this concern over the fact that there are now too many people for civilization to remain human that provides the first of the many strands transforming *Brave New World* into something much deeper than a purely satirical account of the dehumanizing effect which science, in 1932, seemed likely to have on society. In creating a culture where human growth is deliberately stunted in the embryo in order that 'ninety-six identical twins' can work 'ninety-six identical machines', the science of *Brave New World* has merely responded to a problem created by the Ford whom Huxley found he so much admired when faced with the teeming poverty of India. Babies who come out of test-tubes naturally do so in exactly the numbers, size and type required to keep society stable, and Huxley's picture of a world wholly under human control appears at first sight to be the success story of all time. It is only on reflection that one realizes that the problems of human society have been solved in *Brave New World* in the only way that so deeply pessimistic a thinker as Huxley can really envisage: by the removal from human life of those qualities which make man different from the animals. Nobody is allowed to have children of their own, and the words 'mother' and 'father' have become the ultimate in unmentionable obscenity. People are indeed prevented from 'breeding themselves into subhuman misery'.[3] But at the same time, they are refused any opportunity to plan their own lives, educate their own children, possess or transmit their own property, change their role, rank or employment in society, or even live permanently with another person of their own choice. Both physical and mental unhappiness have disappeared. But so too have art, religion, freedom, philosophy and poetry. The risks inseparable from man's ability to breed, to fight, to think up new ways of organizing his society, of persecuting his fellows or blowing himself to pieces, the dangers inherent in life as it naturally exists on a biological level or as man has made it through his invention of society, have been judged too great. 'Anything for a quiet life' is the basic and consciously formulated slogan of this society in which the idea of 'repressive tolerance' is put into practice with quite remarkable success. People are not only bred and conditioned to love their slavery. Any public expression of discontent is quietly put down by a police force which vaporizes the rioters with a 'euphoric, narcotic, pleasantly hallucinant' drug called soma.

There are, nevertheless, some important differences between Huxley's picture of the affluent society and the views which Herbert Marcuse and others were to put forward some thirty years after the publication of *Brave New World*. Whereas the theoreticians of the new left invariably presuppose, in their denunciation of a consumer-orientated society, that freedom and equality have been deliberately destroyed by some kind of nefarious conspiracy on the part of international capitalism and the share-holders of Marks and Spencers, Huxley's critique has no political overtones. It is the impersonal pressure of population and industry, it is man's succes in his most laudable activities of eliminating disease and relieving poverty – making two blades of grass grow where only one grew before – that have made him put himself in this inhuman situation. *Brave New World* is unique in Huxley's work by its complete lack of moral indignation and its absolute ethical neutrality. Nobody is to blame, and there are no villains. Moreover, when one looks at the picture

D

of human experience presented in Huxley's other novels, as well as in historical works such as *Grey Eminence* or *The Devils of Loudun*, the arguments put forward in defence of this benevolently administered world seem neither wholly ironic nor totally unconvincing.

It is indeed in its relationship with Huxley's work and his general personality that much of the peculiar excellence and particular fascination of *Brave New World* are to be found. Its individual themes, of course, are not new. They are announced at various points in the early novels, had been developed by other thinkers in the immediate post-war period, and are in many cases more consistent with the avowedly satirical nature of the work than with its ambiguous portrait of how human beings solve their problems by ceasing to be human. Mr Scogan, in *Crome Yellow*, evokes a future in which 'an impersonal generation will take the place of Nature's hideous system'. 'In vast state incubators', he continues, 'rows upon rows of gravid bottles will supply the world with the population it requires. The family system will disappear; society, sapped at its very base, will have to find new foundations; and Eros, beautifully and irresponsibly free, will flit like a gay butterfly from flower to flower through a sunlit world', and every one of his predictions is made to come true in *Brave New World*. Francis Chellifer, in *Those Barren Leaves*, arguing that stability can be achieved only in a society where the ideal working man is 'eight times as strong as the present day workman, with only a sixteenth of his mental capacity', defends the use of what Huxley later calls dysgenics to avoid the problems of natural intelligence, and thus anticipates the rigid caste system created in A.F. 632.[4] The portrait in *Brave New World* of a society wholly dominated by applied science had also been anticipated outside Huxley's own work by Bertrand Russell, one of the models for Mr Scogan, in a book he had published in 1931 entitled *The Scientific Outlook*. Like Huxley, Russell had insisted on the incompatibility between a rationally organized society and any form of art or literature, and argued that the general public would, in such a society, be forbidden access to works like *Hamlet* and *Othello* 'on the grounds that they glorify private murder'. He had also observed how Pavlov's experiments could be extended to create conditioned reflexes in human beings, and the character training in Huxley's brave new world mirrors Russell's diagnosis of how behaviourism could prevent 'lower-caste people wasting the Community's time on books'.[5] The first sight which the Deltas have of print and pictures is accompanied by violent noises and a mild electric shock, and just as Pavlov, by consistently ringing a bell every time he gave the dog its dinner, managed to make the animal salivate by the bell alone, so the administrators in *Brave New World* ensure that the vulnerability of the human mind can be put to some practical purpose. Indeed, so much of *Brave New World* resembles

The Scientific Outlook that one wonders at times if Huxley put any original ideas into his book.

This charge of plagiarism, however, does not apply either to Huxley's knowledge of science or to the relationship between *Brave New World* and the deeper levels of his personality. In 1963, writing in the *Memorial Volume* which he edited after his brother's death, Sir Julian Huxley went out of his way to discount rumours that Aldous's knowledge of biology always came to him at second hand. 'Most people seem to imagine', he wrote, 'that Aldous came to me for help over the biological facts and ideas he utilized so brilliantly in *Brave New World* and elsewhere in his novels and essays. This was not so. He picked them all up from his miscellaneous reading and from occasional discussions with me and a few other biologists, from which we profited as much as he.'[6] Moreover, what one might call the main philosophical theme in *Brave New World* is a very personal element in the novel, and its emotional impact stems from the fact that Huxley, perhaps without fully realizing what he was doing, made use of the apparently impersonal *genre* of a science fiction fantasy to express a deeply felt personal dilemma. 'A world in which ideas did not exist would be a happy world', he wrote in 1954 in his preface to Krishnamurti's *The First and Last Freedom*, and the remark is strikingly similar to the views which the Director of Hatcheries and Conditioning puts forward in the opening chapter of *Brave New World*: 'Particulars, as everyone knows, make for virtue and happiness; generalities are intellectually necessary evils. Not philosophers, but fret-sawyers and stamp collectors compose the backbone of society.'[7] The dilemma with which Mustapha Mond confronts the Savage when he has to justify the absence from the brave new world of Shakespeare, the Bible, all imaginative literature and all disinterested scientific inquiry is a real one, and the answer proposed in *Brave New World* loses its irony when placed in the context both of Huxley's early work and of his later, mystical development. Since only unhappy people produce literature, and unhappiness itself is so intense, certain and widespread, might it not be a good idea to accept that literature will disappear if suffering is abolished? Since human life requires such misery if the specifically human activities of art and science are to continue, might it not be preferable to end the requirement whereby man must live an animal existence on human terms? Why not, by removing the human element, move him nearer to the animals, and thus destroy the unhappiness which has so far been the unjustifiably high price which he has had to pay for being human?

This kind of question is not one which literature normally asks. Not only is it too naïve, but the problem of inserting it into a convincing account of how people actually behave is quite insuperable. In *Point Counter Point*, for example, as in *Les Chemins de la*

Liberté, The Brothers Karamazov or *Last Exit to Brooklyn*, the very suggestion that people could be happy if they tried is as ridiculous as the idea that they might all suddenly levitate or start to play cricket. The suggestion could only be seriously developed in a work benefiting from the science fiction convention that all things logically possible are also technically feasible. Huxley's exploitation of science fiction as a medium for the expression of ideas provides, in this respect, perhaps the final step in the acquisition for this *genre* of its literary *lettres de noblesse*. It was not only for its concision, social relevance, dramatic qualities, scientific ingenuity and technical expertise that *Brave New World* deserved the signal honour of bridging the two cultures gap by receiving an enthusiastic review from Joseph Needham in F. R. Leavis's *Scrutiny* while at the same time being described as 'a very great book' by Charlotte Haldane in *Nature*. Huxley had also, in his shortest novel since *Crome Yellow*, cast the personal dilemma which runs through his whole work into the highly general medium of a novel about the future. What he asked, over and above the question about the incompatibility between art and happiness, was whether human life could be lived on human terms, or whether the biological accident which gave man his unique status as a suffering, thinking and imaginative being should in some way be rectified. 'So you claim', remarks the World Controller when the Savage insists on contracting out of the 'brave new world' of which he has heard so much, 'the right to grow old and impotent; the right to have syphilis and cancer; the right to have too little to eat; the right to be lousy; the right to live in constant apprehension of what may happen tomorrow; the right to catch typhoid; the right to be tortured by unspeakable pains of every kind?' When the Savage takes a deep breath and says 'I do', the World Controller's ironic 'You're welcome to it' seems to be Huxley's own comment on such obvious lunacy.

It is true that there were, in *Nature* rather than in *Scrutiny*, doubts as to whether the question was altogether fairly put, and whether the complex emotional impulses inspiring *Brave New World* did not spoil what ought to have been an objective analysis of social and scientific problems. Thus Mrs Haldane did not limit herself to anticipating the pill and querying the degree of prescience which Huxley had shown in equipping his young ladies with 'so primitive a garment as a Malthusian belt stuffed with contraceptives when a periodic injection of suitable hormones would afford ample protection'.[8] She also commented, in terms which her husband later regarded as revenge for the satirical portrait given of him under the character of Shearwater in *Antic Hay*, upon the dual personality which, in her view, spoilt the balance in all Huxley's novels. 'Dr. Jekyll and Mr. Hyde', she wrote, 'are nothing to Dr. Huxley and Mr. Arnold. Mr. Arnold is always doing it. He did it in *Point*

Counter Point; he does it in *Brave New World*. Dr. Huxley, who knows and cares about biology and music, science and art, is again ousted by this double of his, this morbid, masochistic, medieval Christian,' and she saw the ending of the novel, in which the Savage commits suicide, as exemplifying the triumph of the Arnold over the Huxley spirit. Yet the Huxleys were no less afflicted than the Arnolds with the metaphysical concerns which Mrs Haldane clearly regarded as the function of science to dispel, and Joseph Needham went so far as to argue that it was precisely Huxley's awareness of how limited the purely scientific attitude could be which made the book so uniquely valuable. What gave the biologist a 'sardonic smile as he reads it', he declared in his review of *Brave New World* in *Scrutiny*, 'is the fact that he knows that *the biology is perfectly right*'. 'Successful experiments are even now being made', he continued, 'in the cultivation of embryos of small mammals *in vitro*, and one of the most horrible of Mr. Huxley's predictions, the production of low-grade workers of precisely identical genetic constitution from one egg, is perfectly possible.'[9] Moreover, he continued, Huxley's novel was invaluable as a description of the kind of society likely to be produced by scientists blind to any values whose existence could not be proved by laboratory experiment. It was, in short, an object lesson for the logical positivists who followed the early Wittgenstein in rejecting statements about ethics, aesthetics and religion as 'meaningless', and a particular warning to scientists of what might happen to them as well as to other people if their more enthusiastic disciples won.

This denunciation of the effect which scientific intolerance could have on society is undoubtedly one of the more conscious and deliberate aspects of *Brave New World*. When Huxley made Francis Chellifer, in *Those Barren Leaves*, remark that his father's Wordsworthian statements about nature were 'as meaningless as so many hiccoughs', he was already treating the cruder interpretations of the *Tractatus Logico-Philosophicus* in a half satirical light, and there is no ambiguity whatsoever about Huxley's later defence of art and literature against the new philistinism of applied science. The same is true of his attack on Freudianism, and here again the themes of *Brave New World* can be traced back to his earlier novels and short stories. Thus in *The Farcical History of Richard Greenow*, the friend who tries to psychoanalyse Richard by the free association technique favoured by the earlier Freudians receives the answer 'bosom' in response to the stimulus 'aunt' (Richard remembers playing with toy soldiers while sitting on his aunt's lap) and that of Wilkinson in response to the stimulus 'God' (there floats into Richard's inward eye 'the face of a boy he had known at school and at Oxford, one Godfrey Wilkinson, called God for short'). The amateur analyst consequently infers that Richard's troubles lie in the fact that he 'had had, as a child, a great Freudian passion for his aunt; and that later on, he had had another passion, almost religious in its fervour, for someone called Wilkinson', and his complete failure to understand what is really happening to his friend foreshadows the criticism that Huxley made much later on, in 1963, in an essay called *Human Potentialities*. There, he wrote of Freud as the man 'who never mentioned any part of the human body except the mouth, the anus and the urethra',[10] and his basic objection really changed little in the forty years separating *The Farcical History* from *Human Potentialities*. The Freudians are wrong because they take into account only one aspect of human physiology, and base their conclusions upon only one kind of evidence: that which emanates from the supposed working of the unconscious in a primarily sexual context. In *Brave New World* it is more the implied ethical teachings of Freudianism that attract his scorn, the rejection of complex and mature emotions in favour of instant gratification and the pleasure principle. His disapproval is, in fact, almost Victorian in its moral intensity, thus revealing yet another apparently contradictory strand in the complex personality of a writer whose work was regarded by *The Times*, in 1963, as having been 'devoted in the main to the violent demolition of Victorian and Edwardian values'.[11]

Thus in *Brave New World* it is the declared aim of the authorities to translate into the sexual behaviour of adults the total irresponsibility and immaturity which supposedly characterize a child's attitude to its own body. 'When the individual feels, the community reels' is the slogan which explains why promiscuous sex is so actively encouraged, and Huxley's insistence upon this theme was another aspect of the novel which, while boosting its sales and encouraging the Australian authorities to act as his publicity agents by banning the book,[12] attracted praise from Joseph Needham, who wrote in *Scrutiny*,

> Whether consciously or not Mr. Huxley has incorporated the views of many psychologists, e.g. Dr. Money Kryle. In an extremely interesting paper Dr. Kryle has suggested that social discontent, which has always been the driving force in social change, is a manifestation of the Oedipus complex of the members of society, and cannot be removed by economic means. With decrease of sexual taboos, these psychologists suggest, there would be a decrease in frustration and hence of that aggression which finds its outlet in religion, socialism or the more violent forms of demand for social change.

Huxley did not, in fact, need to get this idea from Dr Kryle. One of the principal themes in his own early novels is that it is much better to make love than war, and much less harmless to be a lecher than an idealist. The critical presentation of sexuality in *Brave New World* is consequently more of an indication of the general direction which his own ideas were taking than the sign of yet another intellectual debt, and his next two major works, *Eyeless in Gaza* and *Ends and Means*, mark a revulsion both against sexuality and against the total rejection of all conventional values which had characterized the early novels. The founder of the civilization described in *Brave New World* always chose to call himself, 'whenever he spoke of psychological matters, "our Freud" rather than "our Ford"', and it is doubtless as a tribute to the attitude he thus epitomized that all opportunities are taken to prevent emotional tensions building up to the point where they threaten the stability of society. The family, together with all its attendant conflicts, has been replaced by the breeding bottle and the state nursery. At the same time, the universal availability of contraceptives, together with the inculcation, in early childhood, of the duty to be promiscuous, has fulfilled Miss Triplow's prediction in *Those Barren Leaves* and 'made chastity superfluous'. All the adult emotions traditionally associated with sex – love, fidelity, a sense of responsibility, the recognition of another person as supremely and uniquely valuable – have been abolished. All that remains is a search for purely physical pleasure, with T. S. Eliot's 'pneumatic' providing the only adjective of commendation available to describe a woman's charms. If the contraceptives should fail to work, the flood-lit abortion centre in Chelsea provides a ready alternative; and the 'Pregnancy advisory centres' so liberally advertised in the London of 1972 provide yet another example of how some of Huxley's prophecies are being fulfilled more quickly than he expected.

The Freudian idea that we should avoid repressions and frustrations, that the way to happiness lies in the satisfaction of those primitive, instinctual, sexual drives which previous societies have been compelled to inhibit, is thus criticized first and foremost for the effect that it has on people's emotional life. Although he does not specifically mention it, one of the 'established spiritual values' whose importance Huxley rediscovered at the end of *Jesting Pilate* was a belief in monogamy and what one is almost tempted to call romantic love. In *Brave New World* Bernard Marx would like to spend the day alone with his loved one Lenina, walking by themselves in the Lake District, and this almost Wordsworthian attitude to nature, presented in *Those Barren Leaves* in an essentially comical light, is another sign of how Huxley's attitudes were changing. In *Brave New World*, however, the constant reduction of adult human beings to childlike animals is also associated with the deliberate destruction of all intellectual curiosity, and it is difficult to tell whether it is the stunting of the emotions or the prostitution of the mind which Huxley finds most abhorrent. In 'After Ford (or Freud) 632', the only criteria by which society judges itself are those of stability and efficiency. Free, disinterested, open-ended research is consequently regarded as being just as dangerous as art, literature or religion, for the essential characteristic of true scientific inquiry is that no one can know whither it might lead. Each member of society is permitted to know only so much as is immediately relevant to the tasks he has to perform, and even those alpha-plus intellectuals whose pre- and post-natal conditioning has left them with enough intelligence to think for themselves are not allowed to explore any new ideas.

Huxley's realization that the systematic application of technology could lead to a situation where science itself is considered highly dangerous is yet another indication of the fundamental similarity between his attitudes and those of his grandfather. If there was anything to which Thomas Henry Huxley unremittingly devoted his enormous energy, it was the propagation to all members of society of the methods and ideals of scientific inquiry. It was consequently as much by respect for family tradition as through personal taste that Aldous Huxley made this destruction of science by its own hand into an important theme in the actual plot of *Brave New World*, and in this he was quite consciously using a novel about the future to comment on current development in his and our society. The plot revolves round the discovery, by Bernard Marx and Lenina Crowne, of the existence in one of the 'savage reservations' in South America, of Linda, a woman from their own civilization who had been lost some twenty years earlier during an outing very similar to their own. By an unfortunate and almost incredible accident, Linda's excursion among the Pueblo Indians had coincided with her getting pregnant by her lover – now Director of World Hatcheries. By an ironic reversal of traditional standards, it is the very fact that she has had a baby which has prevented her from appealing to her own civiliza-tion for help, and she has been forced to bring up her son alone. When he had asked questions – 'How did the world begin?', 'What are chemicals?' – Linda had been totally unable to reply. The only book she had ever heard of was her own work manual on *The Chemical and Bacteriological Conditioning of the Embryo. Practical Instructions for Beta Workers* and all she knew of chemicals was that they came out of bottles. It is by the quality of the human beings it produces that a civilization can be judged, and it is in the character of Linda that we see what the inhabitants of *Brave New World* are really like and what our own culture might become if the pressures for wholly vocational education are allowed to triumph. They have lost all their adaptability, all their ability and willingness to under-stand other people, all sense of wonder and curiosity, and all power to withstand, in loneliness and isolation, the human experiences of being persecuted or facing death. In his early novels, Huxley seemed to many critics to have followed his grandfather's iconoclastic example and destroyed any Victorian values still left standing after Thomas Henry had so convincingly demolished their religious foundations. In *Brave New World* it is not only the implied insistence on the importance of marriage and pre-marital chastity which suggests that he is going back to what was best in both the agnostic and the Protestant traditions of Victorian England. Education, he implies, must involve more than a vigorous intellectual training in the arts and sciences. Children must also learn to bear misfortune with courage, and to postpone their pleasures until they can face up to their responsibilities. Sexual permissiveness, intellectual conformism and social stability may perhaps lead to a more efficient and comfortable society than has ever existed in the past. But on no account must they be preferred to the ideals of responsibility and self-reliance which have so far characterized the essentially Protestant tradition of Western democracy.

Matthew and even Thomas Arnold would, in this respect, have felt just as much sympathy as Thomas Henry Huxley for the character depicted with most approval in *Brave New World*. Helmholtz Watson, whose lectures on Advanced Emotional Engineering are much admired both by his students and the Authorities, decides to opt out of the comfortable world of an alpha-plus literary intellectual and chooses instead to undergo the rigours of life on an isolated island. There, he will at least have the opportunity of thinking his own thoughts, even though the fact that he does so in conditions of intellectual quarantine will effectively prevent him from influencing what goes on elsewhere. What is equally significant, however, is that the character who more convincingly represents Huxley himself, Bernard Marx, finally lacks the strength of character needed to support loneliness and exile. Like Philip Quarles, Bernard Marx is an alpha-plus intellectual with a physical defect. The rumour runs that 'somebody made a mistake when he was still in the bottle – thought he was a gamma and put alcohol into his blood surrogate', and Bernard consequently suffers from the same feelings of personal inadequacy which characterize all Huxley's autobiographical figures. By tastes and instinct, he resembles the inner-directed man of the Protestant tradition. Yet because of his physical defect, he lacks the psychological qualities which would enable him to fight successfully against the outer-directed, managerial society in which he lives. The self-confidence emanating from the public careers of the earlier generation of Arnolds and Huxleys has disappeared. What takes its place, in *Brave New World*, is not only a fuller realization of how physiological accidents can destroy moral stamina. There is also a more disturbing awareness of how ambiguous certain kinds of moral behaviour can be, and of how preferable an attitude of critical detachment might consequently become. It is never long, in *Brave New World*, before what appears to be

a straightforward attack on contemporary trends takes on more
ambiguous overtones and what W. H. G. Armytage, in *Yesterday's
Tomorrows*, classifies as the product of a 'disenchanted mechano-
phobe' reveals more disturbing if more interesting implications.

In the eighteenth century, and especially in the *Contes* of Voltaire
or Diderot, the role of the outsider in fiction was fairly easily defined.
It was to provide, by the introduction of the common sense supposedly prevailing elsewhere, a criticism of the nonsensical principles
on which modern, European civilization was based. There is also an
outsider in *Brave New World*, Linda's son John, who is rescued from
the savage reservation and brought to London by Bernard Marx,
and it is his reactions to the marvellous world which he has heard
about from his mother which provide the main story line in the
novel. By a happy accident, his reading has not been limited to *The
Chemical and Bacteriological Conditioning of the Embryo. Practical
Instructions for Beta Workers*. He has also read one of the forbidden
works of AF 632, *The Complete Works of William Shakespeare*, and
it is by the standards of Shakespearian tragedy and romance that he
judges the society which finds him so delicious and stimulating a
novelty. Lenina Crowne seems to him the most beautiful and perfect
creature he has ever seen, and he falls madly and devotedly in love
with her. But instead of going to bed with her straight away as the
other young men of her acquaintance have all been conditioned to
do in such circumstances, the Savage behaves very oddly. He insists
on her fitting in not only with *Romeo and Juliette* but with the even
more extraordinary concepts he has absorbed from the fertility rites
and initiation ceremonies of the Pueblo Indians. When she cannot
understand what he is talking about – and she is quite incapable of
imagining that anyone else's frame of reference could possibly be
different from hers – John seeks refuge in an isolated and abandoned
air-lighthouse on the Hog's Back. There, revolted by the spectacle
of a society from which all effort, skill, sympathy and patience have
been removed, he tries to go back to nature and live by his own
efforts. Less rationally, he also tries to whip his body into an
acceptance of the chastity which the memories of Lenina's charms
make into an impossible ideal, but in AF 632, any deviation from the
norm, and especially one with such intriguing sexual overtones,
attracts crowds of spectators. Lenina is among them, and tries to
come and talk to John. But the Savage, already 'frantically, without
knowing it', wishing that the blows he is giving his own body were
raining down on Lenina, strikes at her with his whip. She stumbles
and falls, and as he strikes again and again 'at his own rebellious
flesh, or at that plump incarnation of turpitude writhing in the
heather at his feet', events get out of hand in a way that gives
Huxley's attempt to revive the moral values of nineteenth-century
England some disquieting overtones. The crowd of spectators 'drawn

by the fascination of the horror of pain and, from within, impelled by that habit of cooperation, that desire for unanimity and atonement, which their conditioning had so ineradicably implanted in them', begin to imitate his gestures. Soon, John's search for purity has turned into a sado-masochistic sexual orgy; and the outsider who, in an age more certain of its values, would have represented triumphant sanity, hangs himself in despair.

Another possible if less dramatic sign of the ambiguous attitude which Huxley encourages his reader to adopt towards the society described in *Brave New World* is the extremely humane provision made for those who wish to explore heterodox ideas. When Helmholtz Watson goes off to think his own thoughts, write his own books and perhaps even invent his own God, no one will be allowed to interfere with him. He will, to use Isaiah Berlin's distinction in *Two Concepts of Liberty*, be endowed with all the negative freedom that a man can desire. What he will not have, however, is what Isaiah Berlin calls positive freedom: the opportunity to try to impose his own will on the outside world. The 'repressive tolerance' of consumer orientated society is indeed fully consistent both with certain forms of intellectual freedom and with the behaviour of those individuals who feel that their first duty is towards themselves. What it does not and cannot allow is any changes in its own fundamental patterns. Huxley seems almost to be recommending the *Brave New World* solution as the correct one when he writes, in the opening chapter of *The Perennial Philosophy*, of the way in which 'provision was and still is made by every civilized society for giving thinkers a measure of protection from the ordinary stresses and strains of social life. The hermitage, the monastery, the college, the academy and the research laboratory; the begging bowl, the endowment, the patronage, and the grant of tax-payers' money – such are the principal devices that have been used by actives to conserve that rare bird, the religious, philosophical or scientific contemplative.'[13] Whereas Thomas Henry Huxley – like his other grandson Julian – was a man of action as well as an intellectual, a teacher and administrator as well as an author who helped to change man's concept of his nature, Aldous Huxley limited himself for most of his life to sitting in a room and writing books. Each of the devices he mentions in *The Perennial Philosophy* is characterized by the assumption that the thinker will be neither expected nor allowed to emerge from his ivory tower and play a role in the society that subsidizes his production of ideas, and the islands to which the authorities of *Brave New World* exile their deviant intellectuals would have suited Huxley down to the ground. It was nevertheless in the years immediately following the publication of what still remains his most successful work that Huxley ceased to be what he himself later described as an 'amused, Pyrrhonic aesthete'[14] who stood aside from the world and laughed. For all their gloom and violence, the thirties were still to some extent a time of hope, and the very acuteness of the crisis through which Western society was passing created a future that still seemed to be relatively open. Huxley was one of the many intellectuals and writers who then tried to play an active part in politics and avoid the horrors which, for those who read it in the forties, made *Brave New World* seem even more like a paradise.

5 Pacifism and conversion

The four years separating the publication of *Brave New World*, in January 1932, from the appearance of his next novel, *Eyeless in Gaza*, in July 1936, witnessed a fundamental change in Huxley's work and attitudes. In many ways, *Brave New World* was not only the last and best of what Robert Graves calls the 'novels of disillusion'. It also remains Huxley's funniest book, and the one in which he best realized the brilliance attributed to the Knopescotch of *Crome Yellow*. The world in which the headmistress of Eton is a 'freemartin' called Keate, where the Director of Hatcheries shows his strict observance of social etiquette by giving Lenina Crowne a playful tap on the bottom as he walks past, and where the staid Athenaeum to which all the Huxleys belonged has become the Aphroditaeum, is still the world of schoolboy and undergraduate wit that gave Huxley's first novels their initial charm and permanent appeal. There are also a number of other respects in which *Brave New World* is more a novel of the twenties than of the thirties, and Huxley's prematurely optimistic remark, in *Do What You Will*, that in 'the most fully industrialized countries the Proletariat is no longer abject; it is prosperous, its way of life approximates to that of the bourgeoisie'[1] is an assumption that underlines the whole presentation of the problems of affluence in AF 632. By the time this novel was published, however, the Wall Street crash of 1929 had made both Huxley and others realize that it was perhaps too early to worry about what would happen when society had solved its economic problems. The revolution which brought Hitler to power in Germany in 1933 also showed Huxley that the war which he presented, in *Brave New World*, as happening round about 2090 – and thus ushering in the world peace established in AF 150 – was nearer than he thought. It was this realization that governed all the books that he published from 1936 onwards.

In one of his early essays, *Sermons in Cats*, Huxley speaks of going to the South Sea Islands in order better to study the sexual behaviour of the inhabitants of Mayfair, and a similar desire to understand a complicated system by reference to a simple one seems to have inspired the trip which he took in 1933 to the West Indies and Central America. Indeed, he remarked in the book of essays which he published on his return, *Beyond the Mexique Bay* (1934), that 'Central America, being just Europe in miniature and with the lid off, is the ideal laboratory in which to study the behaviour of the Great Powers', and the general conclusions which he drew from his

observations were almost uniformly pessimistic. As far as Western
Europe was concerned, the only remedy for nationalism, for what
he called the 'set of passions rationalized in terms of a theology'
which prevented men from ever seeing where their true interests lay,
was to be found in the somewhat doubtful hope that the threat of
Hitler's Germany and Stalin's Russia might have the same effect as
the appearance of the great black crow had on Tweedledum and
Tweedledee. Only fear, Huxley suggests, is likely to make men act
more sensibly, and no trust can be placed either in their intelligence
or innate goodness.[2] However, just as Huxley's great charm of
manner and capacity for friendship bore out the truth of Lawrence's
remark that the 'Aldous that writes these novels is only one little
Aldous among others – probably much nicer – that don't write
novels', so Huxley's public actions in a wider context apparently
belied the complete despair about political matters which otherwise
seemed to be the only possible conclusion to be drawn from his
account of human behaviour in the lunatic atmosphere of Central
American nationalism. In June 1935, together with Vera Brittain,
Rose Macaulay, Lord Ponsonby, Brigadier-General F. P. Crozier
and some seven thousand other people, he was present at the Albert
Hall for the initial signing of Dick Shepherd's Peace Pledge Union
renouncing the use of war in all its forms. He also overcame his
dread of the public platform and gave a number of speeches in
favour of pacifism, as well as defending its practices and principles
in books, articles and letters to the newspapers. In April 1936 he
brought out his Pamphlet *What Are You Going To Do About It?*
(drawing from the then Communist poet Cecil Day Lewis the mis-
leadingly illiterate reply *We're Not Going To Do Nothing About It*)
and in July 1937 edited an *Encyclopedia of Pacifism*. Huxley remained
a convinced pacifist to the end of his life, making the case for non-
violence into one of the main themes in *Ends and Means* in 1937 and
arguing in 1946, in *Science, Liberty and Peace*, that non-violent
resistance was the only valid response to the problems of post-war
international politics.

A horror of war had of course been implicit in Huxley's work
from the very beginning. 'Make love not war' is a lesson that not
even his increasingly puritanical attitude towards sex can prevent
emerging from the whole of his work, and it may well be that the
obsession with sado-masochism which becomes increasingly evident
in his fiction from the mid nineteen-thirties onwards is the obverse
side of his horror of physical suffering. In the nineteen-thirties, his
defence of pacifism was more rationally formulated than it had been
in his early work, and consisted of a number of arguments which
demand and deserve an answer. Just as Julian Huxley observes, in
his *War as a Biological Phenomenon*, that intra-specific aggression is
peculiar to men and by no means a 'natural' phenomenon, so

Aldous begins the 'case for constructive peace' in *What Are You Going To Do About It?* by refuting the view that man is condemned by his own bloodthirsty nature to murder his fellows. He has equally little difficulty in showing that violence does not improve matters, and in citing examples of how the methods of 'what may be called combative pacifism' were successfully practised by such leaders as William Penn and Gandhi. In more recent history, the success of the Germans in simply refusing to cooperate with the French during the punitive occupation of the Rhineland in 1923 provided him with an almost perfect example of how non-violent resistance could still be used, and he was also not alone in considering that much of the international discontent of the nineteen-thirties stemmed from the injustice of the Versailles settlement of 1919. The way to remedy this situation, in Huxley's view, was to call an international conference which would 'work out a scheme of territorial, economic and monetary readjustments for the benefit of all', and there is no doubt that this solution, to the eye of reason, was infinitely preferable to any alternative suggested at the time.[3]

Moving from biology and politics to philosophy and ethics, Huxley also pointed out that a rejection of violence formed an essential part of all world religions. In claiming that this was also the case for Christianity, he found himself arguing – in the columns of *The Times* and in letters dated from the Athenaeum – against the Bishop of Durham's insistence that Christians could take part in just wars. It was also in *The Times* that Huxley laid great emphasis, in an argument with Wickham Steed, on the dangers inseparable from the idea of 'Collective Security'. Not only was it morally indefensible, Huxley maintained, to drop bombs on defenceless people from the air. A small, highly industrialized country like England would rapidly be 'reduced to chaos' by systematic air attacks, and there was only one conclusion to be drawn from Mr Baldwin's own recognition that 'the bomber will always get through': since there was no choice between all-out pacifism and the destruction of modern civilization, nations which wished to survive must abandon war as an instrument of national policy.[4] Yet however well argued Huxley's case for pacifism was, it did have certain defects. Some of these appeared only in retrospect, as when neither England nor Germany was reduced to chaos by air raids alone. Others were visible even at the time, and there was no need to be a communist to see them.

The first objection lay in Huxley's own conduct. In 1937, declaring that Europe was no place for a pacifist, he went to America, and subsequently settled permanently in California. It was not an action calculated to enhance the prestige of non-violent resistance in the eyes of the Czechs, Poles or Jews, and it undoubtedly enabled Huxley to take a more detached and Olympian view of events than would have been possible if he had stayed in his own country. It may also have been true, as Huxley argued in *What Are You Going To Do About It?*, that 'the absolute refusal of the English to arm their police is one of the reasons why England is so law-abiding a country' and that 'preventive pacifism is employed by doctors when they treat lunatics'. But when the criminal lunatic uses dive-bombers and tanks, arguments by personal analogy cease to apply to the behaviour of nations. Neither, in the event, was Huxley's major argument in *Ends and Means* borne out by what actually happened either during or after the second world war. Both England and America not only used violence and survived. They also created a society which is not noticeably worse, and is in many ways a good deal better, than the one which the Germans were trying to destroy. Cecil Day Lewis's insistence, in 1937, that the real question should be: 'Will the use of violence in this particular concrete situation benefit the majority of persons concerned?' was consequently a comment whose validity was borne out by events.

Huxley's pacifism is obviously related to an idealistic assumption that other people are as open to reason as he is himself. What it also reflects, however, is a tendency to see political events in catastrophically gloomy terms, and his conviction, in 1919, that the triumphant return to power of Lloyd George would bring 'the consequent abolition of parliamentary government', is only the forerunner of some very odd but very characteristic predictions which came later in his career. Thus in March 1940, we find him speculating on what will happen when 'taxation and professional unemployment have destroyed the existing structure of the middle classes in Western Europe' and writing that it 'certainly looks as if an age of tyranny is before us'. In July 1942, he notes from his mother-in-law's letters that 'conditions in France are very hard', and fears that 'the next big 'flu epidemic will kill off all these under-nourished people like flies'. Even America does not seem very safe. 'Blackwater fever', he notes in the same letter, 'which came by 'plane from Africa to Brazil, is spreading rapidly in its new home and might easily obtain a foothold.' Four months later, he writes America is 'on the verge of gasoline rationing', and this after 'the necessity of conserving tyres' has 'reduced all motion to a minimum'. In spring and early summer of 1944, when 'the proletarianization of the bourgeoisie' is proceeding 'on an unprecedented scale', and it is clear that 'nobody but Stalin is going to be allowed to have much say' in the future of Europe, the problems of England can be dealt with only by 'a continued totalitarianism'. In 1945, it is true, the victory of the Labour Party moves him to hope that 'a few years will elapse' before the publishing house of Chatto and Windus is nationalized. Nevertheless, this optimism disappears at the thought that 'mass production, coupled with mass regimentation for export in exchange for food seems to be the ineluctable destiny' of those countries which, like England, 'have made Malthus's nightmare come true'.[5]

That so intelligent a man as Aldous Huxley could be so wrong about political events is in many ways immensely reassuring. Indeed, his statement in May 1945 that 'after the harvest of 1946, Russia will probably be the only power (being in control of Rumania and Hungary) to offer the Germans bread – which will be given, out of the conquered wheatlands, in exchange for political and economic collaboration' is almost consolation enough for one's failure to invest in Abbey Property Bonds rather than in Rolls-Royce. Statements of this kind are, however, a fairly clear indication that Huxley's pacifism stemmed almost as much from despair as it did from an idealistic vision of man's ability to act rationally in a political context. A pacifist, it has been argued, can justify his refusal to use violence only if he is prepared to give up those things for which men have traditionally fought: his life and possessions, his wife and children, his country and his friends. The whole doctrine of 'non-attachment' recommended in *Ends and Means* presupposes that men are not going to regard anything at all as supremely valuable, and is accompanied by a pessimism about immediate events which runs quite counter to the implied belief of the fighting man that he might win. However natural in a pacifist, an attitude which presupposed that men would be acting correctly only when they did not have any strong personal feelings was also a curious view for a novelist to hold, and added considerably to the difficulty which Huxley had already experienced in giving a sympathetic account of everyday living and ordinary human concerns.

From a biographical point of view, *Eyeless in Gaza* is nevertheless the most fascinating if also the most puzzling of Huxley's works. This fascination stems less from its technique of narration, interesting though this may be to the reader unacquainted with earlier experiments in dislocating the conventional time scheme of the novel, than from its subject matter. As the critic of *The Times* rather unkindly observed when it was first published, *Eyeless in Gaza* presents the reader with a kind of *Alice through the Looking-Glass* world in which we see 'characters weeping before they are pricked and punished before they commit crimes',[6] and it is the reader's task to piece together the different periods in Anthony Beavis's life in such a way as to explain how and why he came to adopt the mystical, pacifist views which we see him expressing fairly early on in the novel, but which in fact constitute the final outcome of his occasionally sordid spiritual pilgrimage. This piecing together is not, in fact, a very difficult exercise, and Huxley is too profoundly rational an author to produce the genuine bewilderment engendered by a novel such as William Faulkner's *The Sound and the Fury*. It is the subject matter that sets the real problem, for nowhere else does

E

Huxley mingle fact and fiction so closely or so curiously together. Thus from one point of view, Anthony Beavis is obviously Huxley himself: he loses his mother at the age of eleven, has a father who remarries, is saved by a physical accident from taking part in the first world war, lives a good deal of his life abroad, is very much a member of the English intellectual upper middle class, is intensely interested in ideas, and finally comes to exchange both the life worship of D. H. Lawrence and the agnostic, apparently irresponsible attitude of the early Huxley for a mystical philosophy which leads him to take a public stand in favour of pacifism. Other events in *Eyeless in Gaza*, however, have a less straightforward autobiographical tone, and are yet sufficiently close to some of Huxley's own experiences to invite comparison and arouse speculation.

Thus Anthony Beavis has a friend, Brian Foxe, who suffers as Trevenen Huxley did from a slight stutter and a highly developed sense of duty. Like Trevenen Huxley, he commits suicide in the summer of 1914, and does so in circumstances which, taken in conjunction with some autobiographical remarks in *Ends and Means*, seem to suggest that Huxley now sees some kind of relationship between his own ideas and his brother's death. 'For myself', he wrote in 1936, 'as, no doubt, for most of my contemporaries, the philosophy of meaninglessness was essentially an instrument of liberation. The liberation we desired was simultaneously liberation from a certain political and economic system and liberation from a certain system of morality. We objected to the morality because it interfered with our sexual freedom; we objected to the political and economic system because it was unjust.'[7] Although Huxley is writing, in this passage as elsewhere, essentially from the point of view of an author striving to persuade his contemporaries that a philosophy of meaninglessness can lead only to totalitarianism and war, there is none the less a curious tone of purely personal guilt and self-reproach. This becomes increasingly apparent when the phrase 'we objected to the morality because it interfered with our sexual freedom' is placed by the side of the central incident of *Eyeless in Gaza*.

This describes how Anthony Beavis, urged on by the desire to impress his new-found and sophisticated mistress Mary Amberley, accepts the challenge to seduce Brian Foxe's fiancée, Joan Thursley. He does not, in any real sense of the word, want to do this, and the five words which, as he looks back on life, he sees as the summing up of 'every biography', are most appropriate to describe his behaviour in this episode: *Video meliora proboque*; *deteriora sequor* (I see the best and approve of it; but follow the worst). Not only does he lack the courage to resist what he fully recognizes as the frivolous cruelty inspiring Mary Amberley's challenge. After he has seduced Joan, whose vulnerability is heightened by Brian's idealistic attitude towards sex, he cannot bring himself to tell his friend what has happened, and this even when the two men are on a walking holiday together in the Lake District. It is consequently from a letter which Joan writes to him that Brian learns how fully he has been betrayed by both his fiancée and his friend, and which impels him to commit suicide. Anthony hides the true reasons for his friend's death by burning both Joan's letter to Brian and Brian's farewell letter to him.

It is not that one seriously wonders, on reading this episode, whether Aldous was in any way responsible for Trevenen's death. Admittedly, there is some similarity of age. According to the dates given in the novel, Anthony is twenty-three in 1914, and Aldous was just twenty when Trevenen killed himself. But there is not a scrap of evidence to show that Aldous Huxley's sexual behaviour ever resembled that of his hero, or that he ever displayed the almost incredible lack of moral courage attributed to Anthony Beavis. What is curious, however, is that he should have attributed actions of this kind to a character who is so similar to him in so many other ways. Admittedly, Anthony Beavis is not a novelist. But his *Elements of Sociology*, on which he works for a disconcertingly large number of years, is clearly a work in very much the same vein as *Jesting Pilate* or *Do What You Will*. In his original conception, writes Anthony, it was intended to be 'a vast *Bouvard and Pécuchet*, constructed of historical facts', an 'apparently objective and scientific picture of futility', and the description certainly fits the atmosphere of Huxley's early essays and novels. Anthony now recognizes that this apparently impersonal ambition was aimed in fact at justifying his own mode of life, and here again there is a marked resemblance between the analysis of his behaviour in *Eyeless in Gaza* and what Huxley says about himself in *Ends and Means*. 'Our conviction that the world is meaningless', writes Huxley, 'is due in part to the fact . . . that the philosophy of meaninglessness lends itself very effectively to further.ing the ends of erotic or political passion', and he clearly intends to present both his earlier self and his current hero as deplorable examples of the inevitable misapplication of certain ideas.

In view of what actually happened in August 1914, however, the use of family history in *Eyeless in Gaza* is rather cavalier. The more direct account of Trevenen's death given in Sir Julian Huxley's *Memories* suggests that if anyone could have helped him and did not do so it was Sir Julian himself. By a coincidence which underlines by contrast how relatively sane Aldous was, both his elder brothers were in the same nursing home at the time of the tragedy, with Julian too absorbed in his own problems to realize how seriously his brother was affected. Trevenen had in fact become attracted to one of the housemaids working in the new family home in London, and attempted to educate her 'by taking her out to plays, concerts and lectures'. When this failed to create a situation where he could reasonably envisage marrying her, he committed suicide. And although, as Sir Julian observes, Aldous must have known what had happened and why, he played no part whatsoever in what happened.[8] Aldous Huxley's use of his brother's suicide to adorn an almost Victorian moral tale can also, however, be explained by more aesthetic considerations. Huxley was not, as he freely admitted, a 'congenital novelist'. He had to take materials that lay conveniently to hand, and was almost totally lacking in the ability to make up plots. When his aunt, the Victorian novelist Mrs Humphry Ward was starting on a new novel, she used to re-read Diderot's *Le Neveu de Rameau*. This most magnificent of all portraits of artistic impotence seemed to act, in Huxley's own words, 'as a kind of trigger or release mechanism', and she was able to embark once again on a detailed and complicated narrative in which virtue was rewarded and vice punished. For all the admiration which he made Mr Cardan express for 'the greatest literary specimen'[9] which Diderot's novel offers of the parasite or court buffoon, Huxley never drew quite the same inspiration from *Le Neveu de Rameau*. Instead, he was obliged to turn either to scientific ideas, or to literary models such as Norman Douglas's *South Wind*, or to family history. Trevenen's death lay conveniently to hand, and was also charged with intense emotional memories. It also gave him an opportunity to express, through the imaginative recreation of the events leading to a suicide, something of the personal remorse which he felt for having been the 'amused Pyrrhonian aesthete' which he had now left behind him. His relationship with his father, and the feeling which he undoubtedly had that Leonard Huxley had betrayed the memory of his first wife by marrying again only four years after her death, inspired another aspect of *Eyeless in Gaza*, and one whose autobiographical implications, while more straightforward, are equally intriguing.

A few months after the publication of *Eyeless in Gaza*, in November 1936, Huxley received what must have been, to judge from his reply, a somewhat hurt and angry letter from his stepmother, Mrs Rosalind Huxley. According to this reply, the main inspiration for the character of John Beavis, Anthony's father, lay in literary sources: a poem by Coventry Patmore called *Tired Memory*, and D. H. Lawrence's *The Virgin and the Gypsy*.[10] Yet just as the D. H. Lawrence short story was, as Huxley remarked, based partly on Frieda Lawrence's description of her first husband, the philologist Ernest Weekley, so the source for John Beavis lay rather in Huxley's own memories than in any literary model. As he admitted in his reply to Rosalind Huxley, he had 'quite unjustifiably' made use of 'mannerisms and phrases some of which were recognizably Father's', and the emotional pattern of John Beavis's life follows that of Leonard Huxley so closely that Rosalind Huxley's distress is easy to imagine. Huxley changes only the sex of the two children which

Leonard Huxley had by his second wife, making his half brothers
David and Andrew into two girls, one of whom, following the best
Huxley tradition, becomes a doctor. There is also a physical resemblance between the portrait of John Beavis, with his 'drooping, brown
moustache' and the photograph of Leonard Huxley on the dust
cover of Ronald W. Clark's *The Huxleys*, and John Beavis has all
of what Aldous regarded as his father's incomprehensible passion
for climbing mountains in Switzerland. Yet it is Leonard Huxley's
remarriage which provides both the main similarity with John Beavis
as well as the emotional stimulus which drove Aldous to create what
is, paradoxically, perhaps his most memorable character. The 'taste
for puns and simple jokes' noted by *The Times* obituary when
Leonard Huxley died in early May 1933 moves on to a higher and
more permanent plane when John Beavis suddenly allows 'his most
daring philological joke to come into his mind':

> 'Where on earth is my teeny weeny penis. Or, to be more accurate,
> my teeny weeny *weeny* . . .'
> Anthony was so taken aback that he could only return a blank,
> embarrassed stare to the knowing twinkle his father shot gaily at
> him.
> 'My pencil', Mr. Beavis was forced to explain. 'Penecillus:
> diminutive of *peniculus*: double diminutive of *penis*; which, as you
> know', he went on, at last producing the teeny weeny *weeny* from
> his inside pocket, 'originally meant a tail' . . .
> It was the first time, Anthony was thinking, that his father had
> ever, in his presence, made any allusion to the physiology of sex.[11]

When Leonard Huxley died, Aldous was travelling in Central
America. He consequently did not accompany his brother Julian and
son Matthew to the funeral service at Golders Green Crematorium
which preceded the interment of Leonard Huxley's ashes in the
Watts Memorial Cemetery, and there was perhaps something sym-
bolic in this accidental absence. Ulysses's line 'And the rude son
shall strike the father dead' does not figure among the Shakespearian
quotations which Aldous used to provide titles for his novels, and
the line about Samson being 'Eyeless in Gaza, by the mill with
slaves', with its emphasis on impotence and enslavement, is his one
quotation from Milton. The novel can none the less be seen as the
final, disrespectful tap on the urn in which Leonard Huxley's ashes
lie buried next to those of his first wife, and the line from *Troilus and
Cressida* might well replace the quotation from *Samson Agonistes* if
one wanted to stress the autobiographical nature of this particular
work. Huxley's portrait of John Beavis is indeed only an intensified
version of the attitude towards fathers and fatherhood visible
throughout his work. With the possible exception of Gumbril Senior,

the fathers in all his novels are vain, selfish, pompous and stupid, sharply contrasted with the more sympathetically observed mothers, whose readiness to help other people undoubtedly reflects Aldous's memory of Julia Huxley. As artistic creations, both fathers and mothers tend to come off slightly better than the younger, more intellectually tormented sons, and both Sydney Quarles and John Beavis stick in the mind long after their sons have faded into autobiographical props for Huxley's ideas. Psychologically, however, Huxley's attitude to his father is also reflected in another aspect of his work and ideas. Even when, after the publication of *Antic Hay*, Leonard Huxley wrote what must have been a very aggressively worded letter accusing his son of 'botanizing on his dead mother's grave', Huxley replied in firm but essentially conciliatory terms;[12] and for all the disapproval of Leonard Huxley's ideas and behaviour that can be read into *Those Barren Leaves* and *Eyeless in Gaza*, Huxley never formally rebelled against his father. Had he done so, he might perhaps have cast off something of the amoeba-like tendency which he attributes to Philip Quarles, and which seems to have made it essential for him, at certain periods in his life, to choose another writer and thinker as his spiritual and intellectual mentor. At the time of *Point Counter Point* and *Do What You Will* this mentor was D. H. Lawrence, and *Eyeless in Gaza* is also autobiographical in the tribute which he pays, through the character of John Miller, to the physician and philosopher F. Matthias Alexander. Together with Gerald Heard, with whom Huxley travelled to America on the *Normandie* in spring 1937 and who became one of his closest friends, it was Alexander who took Lawrence's place and had a profound influence on Huxley's attitude to medicine and science.

Anthony Beavis's meeting with the Scottish doctor James Miller in the wilds of South America is the key episode in his conversion to mysticism, and introduces a character who plays much the same role in *Eyeless in Gaza* as Rampion does in *Point Counter Point*. At one point in the novel, Anthony allows himself to be persuaded to accompany an old school friend, Mark Staithes, on a hare-brained venture to organize a revolution in Mexico. Staithes, a character inspired to some extent by André Malraux's *Les Conquérants*, a book whose importance as a diagnosis of the modern revolutionary temperament Huxley was one of the first English writers to recognize,[13] falls and injures his leg. On his way to fetch help, Anthony has the providential good fortune to meet Miller, who saves Mark's life by amputating his leg. What is more important, however, he converts Anthony not only to a belief in non-violence, but also to the principal idea eloquently defended by Dr Alexander in books such as *Man' Supreme Inheritance*, and *The Use of the Self*. Miller is also a passionate vegetarian, and attributes great importance to the effect which diet has on people's ideas. 'I eat like a Buddhist', he tells

Anthony, 'because I find it keeps me well and happy; and the result is that I think like a Buddhist – and, thinking like a Buddhist, I'm confirmed in my determination to eat like one.' Indeed, so great is his belief in the effect of food on thought that he regards 'butcher's meat' as responsible for perverting Christianity itself. 'What's the greatest enemy of Christianity to-day?' he asks, and replies to his own rhetorical question by an attack on what the unenlightened might perhaps regard as a major blessing of modern technology by answering: 'Frozen meat.'

'In the past', he continues, 'only members of the upper class were thoroughly sceptical, despairing, negative. Why? Among other reasons, because they were the only people who could afford to eat too much meat. Now there's cheap Canterbury lamb and Argentine chilled beef. Even the poor can poison themselves into complete scepticism and despair.'

Like Alexander, Dr Miller believes that correct posture will heal disease by preventing the spinal vertebrae from 'grinding together'. He also praises 'colonic irrigation', and the influence on Huxley of those thinkers who attribute almost magical qualities to the various practices of this type is even clearer in his *Letters* than in his novels and essays. Thus in March 1936, he writes to E. McKnight Kauffer to suggest that he too might overcome his insomnia and generally run-down condition by treating the 'chronic intestinal intoxication' which lies at the root of 'millions' of symptoms by a 'course of colonic lavage and the receiving of two injections of a vaccine prepared from the pathogenic organisms found in the faeces'; and in November 1942 he has some equally unusual recommendations to make to his brother Julian. A 'meatless, milkless, saltless' diet of 'beans and other legumes' has, he claims, cured him of 'the trouble in the nervous system, betraying itself in such diverse symptoms as heart irregularity, intestinal spasm, hives, bronchitis, and the continuous falling-off of one of my finger-nails'. He goes on to suggest that 'something along similar lines would be of help in your case'. Other remedies designed to alleviate the ills afflicting what Huxley called 'the body of this death' included, in December 1943, wriggling on a board as a possible cure for skin disease, and in 1950 recommending Julian to keep sinusitis at bay by listening to 'a record of sounds in the lowest musical octave'. In 1957 we find Aldous using nicotinic acid in an attempt to lower the level of cholesterol in the blood, and in 1959 seriously interesting himself in 'a man . . . who has trained his daughter and niece to see without their eyes'.[14]

Huxley did not, it is true, lack reasons for looking favourably on remedies which orthodox medicine might tend to dismiss as belonging to the realm of faith healing. From 1939 onwards, his adoption

of the Bates method for training people with poor eyesight to see
without glasses enabled him to improve his own sight almost beyond
recognition, and he later made a point of ensuring, as a tribute to
Bates's memory, that any advertising material put out by his publisher should show him without the heavy glasses which he had once
been forced to wear. Neither did orthodox medicine endear itself to
him when his son Matthew fell ill as a result of all the 'horse serum'
and sulpha drugs pumped into him when he was briefly enlisted in
the American army in 1942, and the incident moved Huxley to
consider writing 'a little book on fashions in medicine' which would,
he wrote, be 'as extravagantly farcical as that of fashions in
women's clothes'. The preoccupation with medical matters, although
natural in a member of the world's most distinguished family in the
field of biological studies, also reveals Huxley to have been at certain
times in his life almost a professional invalid, and in this he was by
no means unique. His brother Julian seems to have enjoyed equally
bad health, and in this respect both he and Aldous resemble their
grandfather. In 1838, when he was only fifteen, Thomas Henry
Huxley was present at a dissection and absorbed some kind of
poison from which he never wholly recovered. From that time
onwards, he wrote, 'my constant friend, hypochondriacal dyspepsia,
commenced his half-century of co-tenancy of my fleshly tabernacle'.[15]

It is occasionally tempting, especially in view of the date at which
Aldous Huxley began to interest himself in unorthodox ways of
curing his various illnesses, to see his mysticism as a parallel attempt
to obtain rapid results by breaking out of conventional attitudes and
modes of thought. His statement in *Grey Eminence* that 'a totally
unmystical world would be a world totally blind and insane' implies
a complete dismissal of any form of traditional humanism or even
of non-mystical religion, and this attitude towards the efforts which
more conventional thinkers have made to find a basis for human
ethics is echoed in a remark which he made in a letter to Kingsley
Martin in 1939: 'So long as the majority of human beings', he wrote,
'choose to live like the *homme moyen sensuel*, in an "unregenerate
state", society at large cannot do anything but stagger from catastrophe to catastrophe',[16] and an acute pessimism about the behaviour
of men in a social context also seems, to judge from *Eyeless in Gaza*,
to apply to their actions as individuals. This is especially the case for
Anthony Beavis, whose total failure in personal relationships is in
no way limited to the circumstances surrounding his reluctant
seduction of Joan Thursley. Some twenty years after Mary Amberley
blackmails him into betraying his closest and most loyal friend,
Anthony has a more prolonged and physically more satisfactory
affair with her daughter Helen. Here again, however, he allows
vanity and sexual pleasure to come before loyalty to a person he
likes and esteems, for Helen is married to another man he had

known since boyhood, Hugh Ledgwidge, whose interest in books, art and ideas closely mirrors both Anthony's and Huxley's own tastes. Unfortunately, however, Hugh is not very good in bed, and cannot live up to the romantic and passionate letters he had written to Helen during their engagement. Anthony profits from her sexual disillusionment, while constantly refusing to allow more serious emotions to interfere with his egotistical search for sensual pleasure. However, a dramatic incident cuts short what the pagan philosophy of *Do What You Will* might well have regarded as a very satisfactory relationship, and eventually leads Anthony to a position where he seems to give up close personal contacts altogether.

One day, as they are lying naked on the flat roof of Anthony's house in the South of France, Helen and Anthony are suddenly awoken by a 'strange yelping noise' punctuating the din of an aeroplane flying over their heads. A dark shape rushes down towards them, and before they have time to realize what is happening, a fox terrier that had been travelling in the open cockpit of the old-fashioned machine bursts like a bomb on the roof beside them and drenches them both with its blood. In one sense, the absurdly improbable incident is a parody of Christianity. The lovers are 'drenched with the blood of the dog' in the same way that sinners in the past were 'washed with the blood of the lamb'. Such an interpretation would be fully consistent with the tone of remorse that predominates both in *Ends and Means* and in *Eyeless in Gaza*, and would also show an interesting debt on Huxley's part to T. S. Eliot's lines in *The Waste Land*: 'Oh keep the dog far hence that's friend to man Or with his nails he'll dig it up again'. The dog represents, for Eliot, the humanistic attitude which refuses to accept the death of the self which is an integral part of all religions, and Huxley is clearly making the same point about the inadequacies of humanism but in a more dramatic and obvious way. Because Helen and Anthony have lived like animals they are punished by being temporarily united with the least attractive of all the beasts, and the philosophical point which Huxley is making is all the more effective because of the tone of physical disgust which the incident evokes. However, the central place of the incident in the general structure of *Eyeless in Gaza* also emphasizes the revulsion against exclusively human feelings which characterizes the whole book. Even though Anthony suddenly discovers 'all the affection implicit in their sensualties and yet never expressed', and which 'seems to discharge itself in a kind of lightning flash of accumulated feeling, upon this person, this embodied spirit weeping in solitude behind concealing hands', this revelation of the possibilities inherent in human relationships comes too late. All the horror which she had always felt for blood and physical suffering suddenly floods into Helen's mind and fixes itself upon this man with whom she had so often lain 'in a rapt agony of pleasure' on 'that death bed in which he also had his part as assassin and fellow victim'. She cannot bear to touch Anthony, and leaves him. In London, she meets and falls in love with a young German communist, Ekki Giesebrecht. But the intense happiness which she finds with him is suddenly cut short when he is captured by the Gestapo and tortured to death. Only at the end of the novel, when she has begun to recover from her grief, does there seem to be a possibility of her and Anthony coming together again. But if they do, it will be in a world of 'calm of mind, all passion spent', and the Baudelairean 'torture of pleasure' which Helen Amberley, like Lucy Tantamount, experiences in her sexual life remains for ever unsanctified by the human emotions of love, tenderness and concern.

Huxley's conversion to mysticism thus in no way improves the quality of the human relationships studied in his fiction, and *Eyeless in Gaza* differs little in this respect from *Point Counter Point*. This is visible even in such minor characters as Helen's more conventionally minded sister, Joyce, who marries a pleasant young subaltern only to find herself, after a few years in India, 'sickly and gaunt before her time', tied to a resentful husband already 'furtively interested in fresher, plumper bodies'. Even the one character who appears, at first sight, to represent conventional goodness, has a devastating effect on the people around her, and Huxley leaves no doubt as to why Brian Foxe is himself unable to respond to Joan Thursley's natural and spontaneous love. His mother, Rachel, has poured out on him all the love and devotion that her husband had been unwilling to accept, and so filled him with her own, impossibly idealistic brand of Christianity, that he has become an emotional cripple. Anthony's irresponsibility and selfishness may have been the final cause of his death, but he had been killed emotionally long before by the great love his mother bore him. It is not only the adulterous couple lying in the clear, pagan sunlight of the South of France who are spattered with the filth of normal human relationships, and John Miller is clearly a mouthpiece for Huxley's own mystical views when he inveighs against the attention accorded to 'this piddling, twopenny-halfpenny personality, with all its wretched little virtues and vices, all its silly cravings and silly pretensions'. In October 1934, Huxley had written to Mrs Flora Strousse that he was working on 'a difficult novel about the problem of freedom', and it is clear from both the title and the general theme of *Eyeless in Gaza* that this was it. But it is equally clear from the atmosphere and conclusions of the novel that the freedom which the hero finally achieves, and which is presented to the reader as one of the supreme values, is not without its ambiguities.

Thus in so far as it is ultimately based either on a refusal or an inability to become involved with individual people, Anthony Beavis's freedom is very difficult to distinguish from total indifference. He does, it is true, try to get through to Helen after the incident with the dog has shown him that he loves her as a person as well as appreciating her as a sexual partner. But once he fails to make contact with her, he moves away from the plane of personal relationships altogether, abandoning revolutionary politics only for the vaster and more impersonal concerns of pacifism and mystical philosophy. It is easy to free oneself from people, and easy to refuse to fight for them, if one begins by rejecting as pointless most of what they do and feel, and the attitude towards human relationships which emerges both from *Eyeless in Gaza* and from *Ends and Means* reveals an impatience with ordinary life that runs strangely parallel to Huxley's rejection of conventional politics and distrust of ortho- dox medicine. This impatience also casts a certain shadow over the ethical values presented as desirable at the end of *Eyeless in Gaza*, and which form the basis for all Huxley's later thought on social and political questions. On the one hand, Huxley clearly agrees with Miller in seeing no good in human beings as they are now. But at the same time, he makes Miller argue that they must be treated humanely, and with respect, 'as men and not insects', insisting that 'if one looks for men, one finds them. Very decent ones, in a majority of cases'. Every religion, it is true, is built upon a paradox, and a saint could well see human beings both as morally worthless and as infinitely valuable in the sight of God. In the case of a novelist, however, this paradoxical attitude is more difficult to maintain, and the novels which Huxley wrote after his conversion suffered from the difficulties which any artist encounters when working with materials that, with one part of his mind at least, he despises.

There are, however, a variety of possible reasons why Huxley's fiction has never enjoyed a very high reputation with the more literary critics. It may be that they cannot forgive him the know- ledge of science which they lack, and they may find it hard to admire an author who wears his intellect so obviously on his sleeve. This is certainly the view of Mrs Leavis, who delivered a scathing attack on *Eyeless in Gaza* in the September 1936 number of *Scrutiny*. It was, she remarked, no accident that Huxley's two most autobiographical characters, Philip Quarles and Anthony Beavis, were such assiduous note-takers. Their habit of noting down impressions and ideas reflected Huxley's own purely superficial intelligence, and led merely to a series of 'dubious generalizations' that were never integrated into a consistent world vision. Moreover, continued Mrs Leavis, Huxley's 'radical defect as a novelist, his lack of interest in the novelist's raw material, is responsible for his insensitivity to speech and emotional idiom', with the result that his characters are 'defin- able if at all by gross verbal mannerisms'.[17] While these remarks do less than justice to the complex interweaving of themes in *Point Counter Point*, to the use of an unusual time sequence in *Eyeless in*

Gaza, and to the general portrait of the English intellectual upper middle class offered by Huxley's fiction, they do provide another way of looking at the effect which his mysticism had on his performance as a novelist. The reasons for the decline which most critics agree took place after 1936 were in fact also suggested by the description of Anthony Beavis, in *The Times* review of *Eyeless in Gaza*, as 'a worm whose ingeniously intellectual wrigglings do nothing to make more agreeable';[18] for if a novelist can seriously present as a kind of spiritual success story the life of a character who fails in every human relationship he undertakes, then he is surely going against the basic principle lying behind the *genre* he is employing.

Mr Propter, Huxley's mouthpiece in the novel which immediately followed *Eyeless in Gaza*, *After Many a Summer* (1939), waxes eloquent about the inadequacy of 'merely descriptive plays and novels' which contain 'just a huge collection of facts about lust and greed, fear and ambition, duty and affection . . . with no co-ordinating philosophy superior to common sense and the local system of conventions, no principle more rational than simple aesthetic expediency'. Since Huxley also clearly agrees with Mr Propter's assertion that 'on the strictly human level, there is nothing that deserves to be taken seriously except the suffering which men inflict on themselves by their crimes and follies', it is rather surprising that he should continue to write novels. What is even more extraordinary, however, is that some of them should still at times attain the level of excellence which he achieved in his account of the complexities of human experience in *Point Counter Point*, when his idea that life was worth living on a human level was more consistent with the practice of the novelist's craft. It may well be true, as Peter Bowering observes, that Huxley has never 'created a redemptive figure of the sustained depth of Forster's Mrs Moore',[19] and it would in fact have been remarkable, given the ideas lying behind his fiction, if he had done so. But his later novels are by no means as dull as Mr Propter's remarks seem to imply, and his mystical beliefs destroyed neither his wit nor the virulence of his satire.

There are, it is true, other examples of writers whose official view of human beings is inconsistent with the implications underlying prose fiction. Flaubert is a case in point, for the scorn which he expressed throughout his *Correspondance* for human beings as they naturally are did not prevent him from becoming one of the greatest of French novelists. In the case of Huxley, however, the apparent contradiction between his views on humanity and his later aesthetic achievements runs parallel to a more interesting contrast between the self-portrait contained in his fiction and the view which other people had of him; and it is perhaps only in the range of their intellectual curiosity and apparently deplorable habit of taking notes that Philip Quarles and Anthony Beavis really resemble their creator.

Huxley may well have felt instinctively more at home with ideas than with people. But the man who could go on a picnic with Krishnamurti, Charlie Chaplin, Greta Garbo, Bertrand Russell, Paulette Goddard, Christopher Isherwood and Anita Loos – whom he would have liked to keep as a pet, because she was so small – must have had a talent for personal relationships which was as far beyond the reach of most mortals as Huxley's equally legendary talent to discourse on the finding of bacteria at ocean depths, the technical deficiencies of Baudelaire's Latin poems, and the habits of 'what the onomatopeic Mayanas called the Dzunuum'.[20] The number of letters which he wrote to people is also an indication of the extent to which he tended to present the poorest possible image of himself in the autobiographical aspects of his fiction, and it is particularly significant in this respect that Anthony Beavis should have been an only child. Neither he nor Philip Quarles had a brother with whom they were on such consistently good terms as Aldous was with Julian, and the man of whom a woman journalist on *Vogue* could say 'just to have met him was enough to make one's day' was far from being either the bore that Huxley became when he put on his Propter personality or the shrinking, exclusively cerebretonic, shy intellectual with a strong distaste for all personal contacts who emerges from *Point Counter Point* or *Eyeless in Gaza*. For all the attacks which he made, in *The Perennial Philosophy*, on the Christian idea of remorse, Huxley does seem to have gone through quite prolonged spells where he felt guilty for the kind of person he may occasionally have been. Quite why he tried to exorcize this by presenting a very unfavourable picture of himself in his books is difficult to say, and the intellectual masochism which led him to grace Philip Quarles with his own unfailing courtesy only to explain it as a device for avoiding contact with other people remains inexplicable on intellectual grounds. What is certain is that he both cared more for people as individuals than either his novels would suggest or his mystical views imply. The verdict of his Italian housekeeper *Era tanto buono*, recorded by Sybille Bedford as an indication of the esteem which Huxley's 'courtesy, ease and dignity'[21] inspired in everyone who met him, is equally a sign that the view of humanity sometimes expressed in his novels neither affected nor reflected his personal conduct. 'A book is a product of a different self from the one we manifest in our habits, in our society, in our vices', wrote Proust in *Contre Sainte-Beuve*, and if one replaces 'vices' by 'virtues', there are few English writers to whom this remark applies more aptly than to Aldous Huxley.

6 *The Perennial Philosophy*

One of the most surprising features of Aldous Huxley's work and ideas, especially when one remembers the goodness radiating from him in his personal relationships, is a recurrent anti-semitism which shows itself not only in incidental remarks in books and letters but also in his approach to a number of religious, philosophical and historical questions. In this respect he has a distinguished predecessor in Voltaire, who agreed with him in accepting the myth that the Jews possess immense financial power, and who would also have under-written the disapproval expressed both in *Do What You Will* and *Ends and Means* for what Huxley regarded as the characteristic feature of semitic thought: a single-minded devotion to a particular concept of God and history. At the time of Huxley's professed and militant agnosticism, the essentially Jewish idea that there is only one God ran counter to his admiration of the Greeks for their polytheism, for their ability to recognize that 'all the manifestations of life are god-like, and every element of human nature has a right – a divine right – to exist and find expression'.[1] While when he became a mystic, the ritualistic and authoritarian tendencies of Old Testament thinking seemed to him totally opposed to the best traditions of the perennial philosophy, and to the tolerance for different psychological types implied by the 'eight-fold path' of Buddhism.

In *Do What You Will*, Huxley declares with some vehemence that humanity would have been much better off if the Jews had remained 'not forty but four thousand years in their repulsive wilderness'. We should then have avoided, he argues, both the persecuting tendencies inseparable from monotheism and the admiration for worldly success which the Protestant thinkers of the sixteenth century inherited directly from the Old Testament. We should also have been spared the cruelty and intolerance which 'that old-fashioned Hebrew prophet in scientific fancy-dress, Karl Marx' made into an integral part of communism, and should not still be suffering from 'the native incapacity of the Jews to be political', and which made them so incapable of organizing their national life with the same respect for diversity of opinion that characterized the Greek city state. In *Ends and Means*, Huxley elaborates on the implications of this remark, as he deplores the influence on European thought wielded by the Old Testament, that 'history of the cruelties and treacheries of a Bronze-Age people, fighting for a place in the sun under the protection of its anthropomorphic tribal deity',[2] and it is strange how a book written in praise of tolerance should sometimes have so self-righteous a tone.

It is nevertheless not difficult for the student of European history to agree with Huxley that the results of the belief in a God of Battles have been uniformly disastrous, and to appreciate his reasons for seeing Jewish thought as principally responsible both for such 'criminal lunacies' as the religious wars of the sixteenth and seventeenth centuries and for the tendency of Christianity to become the least mystical of the world religions. Because the Jews saw God as standing above and apart from man, Christianity has been suspicious of such mystical thinkers as Eckhart, with his remark that 'God is not good, I am good', or of Ruysbroeck and his view that 'God in the depths of us receives God who comes to us; it is God contemplating God'.[3] For orthodox Christians, in Huxley's opinion, God is wholly separate and different from man, an angry father who must be placated, and a cruel tyrant who demanded the death of his son as a ransom to save mankind from hell. The Eastern religions, which escaped the essentially semitic concepts of monotheism and of an avenging God, have a much more sensible vision of Him. For them, He is both immanent and transcendent, and there can be no question of man fulfilling his religious duties by sacrificing himself to a jealous and angry Father. God is manifest wherever love triumphs over hatred, or when tolerance and non-attachment overcome the self-assertive imperialism which Huxley presents as having been the ruin of European religious thought and political life. Since 'the eye with which God sees us is the same as the eye with which we see him ...' there is no danger in the pure mystical tradition of man alienating himself by his religious beliefs.

The most that can be said in defence of Huxley's more extreme remarks in *Do What You Will* and *Ends and Means* is that they are directed less against the Jews as a race than against a set of mental and spiritual attitudes which he would have found equally objectionable in any group of people. Some of his incidental comments in his letters, such as his remark about having to follow the wishes of 'the all-powerful Jewish gentleman in charge of distribution' whenever one had anything to do with the cinema, are less defensible; while the description in *Do What You Will* of 'those mournfully sagging, sea-sicklishly undulating melodies of mother-love and nostalgia and yammering amorousness and clotted sensuality' as 'the characteristically Jewish contribution to modern popular music' is, to put it mildly, unkind.[4] On a more general level, it is curious to note how, in Huxley's case, the anti-semitism associated in other writers – except, of course, Voltaire – primarily with authoritarian modes of thought such as fascism, reflects a hostility towards any kind of doctrinaire thinking. What he cannot stand about the Old Testament is its exaltation of tradition and authority over the freedom of the

individual to choose his own values and mode of life, and in this he
again resembles his paternal grandfather. There is nevertheless an
important difference between the iconoclasm of *Antic Hay* or *Do
What You Will* and the hostility to authoritarian modes of religious
or political thought in *Ends and Means* or *The Perennial Philosophy*.
The scepticism of Huxley's later period is far more obviously
directed to moral ends, and does not apply either to the taboos on
sexual conduct mocked in *Do What You Will* or to the tenets of
mystical religion dismissed as meaningless in *Jesting Pilate*. 'To
travel', he had written in 1926, 'is to discover that everyone is
wrong.' In *Ends and Means*, in 1937, he declares that 'among human
beings who have reached a certain level of civilization and of personal
freedom from passion and social prejudice, there exists a real *consensus gentium* with regard to ethical first principles'. What is
perhaps rather surprising, in view of the caustic remarks which he
made about mysticism in his earlier career is that he should find this
consensus gentium in the field of religious philosophy. All mysticism
and transcendentalism, he had declared in *Do What You Will*, in
1928, formed part of an attempt to escape from 'the welter of immediate experience'; and he condemned any search for a unified and
consistent world view on the grounds that 'absolute oneness is
absolute nothingness; homogeneous perfection, as the Hindus per-
ceived and courageously recognised, is equivalent to non-existence,
to nirvana'. In 1937, he writes that 'the mystical experience testifies
to the existence of a spiritual unity underlying the diversity of
separate consciousness', and speaks of the 'web of understanding
which, in the mind of the accomplished intellectual, connects the
atom with the spiral nebula and both with this morning's breakfast,
the music of Bach, the poetry of neolithic China, what you will'. The
contrast with the statement in *Do What You Will* that 'a tree, a table,
a newspaper, a piece of artificial silk are all made of wood. But they
are, none the less, distinct and separate objects', could hardly be
greater.[5]

From 1937 onwards, almost everything Huxley published was
directed in some way or other to explaining or exemplifying the
principles of the mystical philosophy which provided him, from
Eyeless in Gaza and *Ends and Means* onwards, with the basis both
for his pacifism and for his apparent confidence that human existence was not simply a biological accident. He did, moreover, differ
from most other writers on mysticism in continuing to express his
ideas with quite exceptional clarity, and even apparently recondite
works such as *The Perennial Philosophy* or *Grey Eminence* are very
much in the tradition established by Thomas Henry Huxley when
he took on the role of Darwin's Bulldog or gave his six lectures to
working men on *Our Knowledge of the Causes of the Phenomena of
Organic Nature*. What the French call *haute vulgarisation* is an

essential part of the Huxley family tradition, and the 'need to inform' which Ronald Clark finds characteristic of Julian Huxley's personality was equally evident in his brother Aldous. Yet none of the works of Huxley's mystical period is free of the same kind of ambiguities which ran through the humanism of *Point Counter Point* and *Do What You Will*, and it is both the task and the privilege of the commentator on his work to draw attention to these. In *Point Counter Point*, Spandrell suggests that this earth might be 'some other planet's hell', and if one is to base oneself, as Huxley insists that he is doing throughout *The Perennial Philosophy*, on the evidence immediately available, it would be difficult to reject the suggestion as just a joke. The account of experience in Huxley's own novels is an indication that Spandrell might well be right, and there is an unsurmountable contradiction between this neo-Dostoievskian vision of human life as a kind of hell and Huxley's other remark about the 'fundamental all-rightness of the world'[6] which he insists is revealed in mystical experience.

In August 1945 Huxley remarked to John Van Druten that *The Perennial Philosophy*, the central and most important work of his mystical period, had been 'very interesting to compile and write', and it is an indication of the interest aroused by Huxley's work in the mid nineteen-forties that over twelve thousand copies were sold before the official publication day in September of the same year. It is an anthology of the views expressed by the mystical writers of both East and West, all illustrating the same basic philosophy: that each person is, in the deepest core of his being, part of the Ultimate Reality of God; that this reality is transcendent throughout the universe as well as immanent in each human soul; and that man's final end consists of knowing himself to be part of this ultimate reality, to the point where his superficial, worldly personality, is totally absorbed into what the *Tibetan Book of the Dead* calls 'the clear light of the void'. Everything which stands in the way of enlightenment, of man's realization that, as Ruysbroeck says, 'the image of God is found essentially and personally in all mankind', is to be avoided. The lusts of the flesh and the pride of life, the negative emotions of hatred and fear, the intolerance stemming from man's tendency to give reality to his own purely verbal accounts of experience, remorse for past acts or longings for private existence must all disappear. What will then remain is the experience of eternity that is available, here and now, to those who realize who they really are and can say 'Not I but God in me.' It is 'the existence at the heart of things of a divine serenity and goodwill' which, writes Huxley, 'may be regarded as one of the reasons why the world's sickness, though chronic, has not proved fatal', and which consequently gives creation a purpose. Indeed, Huxley even turns to evolution itself for evidence to support this point of view. 'It looks as though', he writes, 'in the

F

cosmic intelligence test, all living matter, except the human, has succumbed, at one time or another in its biological career, to assuming, not the ultimately best, but the immediately most profitable form.' Only man is capable of further development, and there is only one direction in which he can go: towards a greater awareness, on the part of more people, that they themselves are 'one of the infinite number of points where divine Reality is wholly and eternally present'. 'Society is good', writes Huxley in his conclusion, 'to the extent that it renders contemplation possible for its members', and he provides what his admirers might well consider as his own best epitaph when he observes, of those who have achieved the ultimate freedom of sainthood, that 'such men not only liberate themselves; they fill those they meet with a free mind'.[7]

The Perennial Philosophy is undoubtedly a fascinating book. It is also, as Aldous's second wife, Laura Archera Huxley, observed, a very beautiful one. The religion it advocates is free of dogma, and could never give rise to persecution. Its moral ideals are both noble and practical, and its social effects could only be good. Whether the book is convincing as philosophy, however, is more open to doubt, and a reviewer in *The Times Literary Supplement* did indeed observe that there was, in the Western sense of the word at any rate, very little 'philosophy' in it.[8] This, of course, was Huxley's own intention. His very first chapter insists on the futility of asking metaphysical questions about the origins of the universe or the underlying reasons for certain events, and he notes approvingly that 'the Buddha declined to make any statement in regard to the ultimate divine Reality'. Mysticism, he wrote in a letter to Dr J. B. Rhine in December 1942, is 'based on direct experience, as the arguments of the physical scientists are based on direct sense impressions', and he describes the Buddha of the Pali scriptures as 'a teacher whose dislike of "footless questions" is no less intense than that of the severest experimental physicist of the twentieth century'.[9] 'Whatever can be said at all', wrote Wittgenstein at the end of the *Tractatus Logico-Philosophicus*, 'can be said clearly. And what we cannot talk about we must consign to silence', and it might perhaps seem, in this respect, that *The Perennial Philosophy* does offer the synthesis between religious experience and the scientific temper which seemed so inaccessible to Thomas Henry Huxley when he helped to demonstrate the incompatibility between the facts of evolution and the legends of Genesis. When the mystic actually experiences the ultimate truth of the universe, argues the Huxley of *The Perennial Philosophy*, there is no need for him to indulge in 'willed assent to propositions known in advance to be unverifiable'. Indeed, since the ultimate Ground 'simply "is"', there are not even any questions to be answered.[10]

This refusal to speculate on such questions as the nature of God, the origins of human life, the meaning of the universe or the causes of suffering would be fully acceptable if Huxley's own vocabulary did in fact avoid all mention of such concepts. But when he writes of 'man's deep-seated will to ignorance and spiritual darkness', he inevitably raises the question of how a being that is not only potentially but actually divine also came to be evil. Similarly, his use of a phrase such as 'man's final end' raises just as many metaphysical questions as the opening question in the catechism of the Presbyterian Church of Scotland which it so much resembles;[11] while the second word in his statement that 'the goal of creation is the return of all sentient beings out of separateness and that infatuating urge-to-separateness which results in suffering, through unitive knowledge, into the wholeness of eternal Reality', also implies a teleological concept of the universe which can only be elaborated in terms of the metaphysical concerns which he has earlier dismissed. It may well be, as Huxley claims in his discussion of Pauline Christianity in the chapter entitled 'Suffering', that the orthodox doctrine of the Atonement is 'the projection of a lawyer's phantasy'.[12] The fact nevertheless remains that the Christian account of the Fall does offer some explanation of why men should be so wicked; and that the doctrines based on the crucifixion do provide a coherent philosophy that can be discussed in intellectually meaningful terms. *The Perennial Philosophy*, in contrast, reminds one at times of the scientist whose views were dismissed by one of his colleagues with the remark: 'This isn't right. It's not even wrong.'

Such objections do, of course, presuppose that the Western tradition of philosophical argument, with its insistence upon logical demonstration and on clear and distinct ideas, is intellectually valid. The praise which Huxley gives to Buddhism is a fairly clear indication that he did not think this was so, and his remark that 'the habit of analytical thought is fatal to the intuitions of integral thinking, whether on the "psychic" or the spiritual level' shows how mistrustful he was of the in-built habits of Western philosophy. It is nevertheless very difficult for a thinker to break away from the philosophical presuppositions inherent in the very language he uses, and Huxley's use of words such as 'goal', 'end' and 'will' shows how fully the basic tools of his trade compelled him to remain a Western intellectual. It is certainly impossible to explain why an infinitely good and merciful God should create human beings simply in order that they might, in due course, be totally reabsorbed in the Ground of all Being, and Huxley's refusal to indulge in metaphysics seems suspiciously like the attitude of a man who refuses to ask questions because he is afraid of the answer he might receive. Once the facts of pain, of cancer, of the pointless suffering inflicted on men and animals are taken into consideration, Spandrell's hypothesis begins to fit the available evidence more appropriately than phrases about the 'fundamental all-rightness of the world' revealed through mystical experience. After all, anyone can feel that this world is another planet's hell; and find plenty of evidence to substantiate his view. A visit to the nearest hospital, a television programme on East Pakistan, a reading of the pages describing little Phil's meningitis in *Point Counter Point*, are enough. Mystical experiences, on the other hand, are vouchsafed only to the few, and Huxley himself is most insistent both that there is no salvation for 'nice, ordinary unregenerate people'[13] and that the number of those prepared for mystical contemplation is very small. Surely, one is tempted to say, the Godhead is as wasteful of the souls that have to keep going on to what the Buddhists call the Wheel of Creation as nature itself is of the 'million, million spermatozoa' which are foredoomed either to perish without fertilizing an ovum or, if they do fulfil their purpose, nowadays merely add to the problem of over-population.

In *Do What You Will* Huxley had explained mystical experiences by saying that they 'happen because they happen, because that is what the human mind happens to be like'. In *The Perennial Philosophy* he is implicitly saying the same thing about physical suffering, and refusing to go any further in case it turns out to be Spandrell rather than the mystics whose vision best fits the facts. 'Your enjoyment of the world is never right', wrote Thomas Traherne in one of the phrases whose presence in *The Perennial Philosophy* are more than adequate compensation for its unsatisfactory metaphysics, 'until every morning you wake in Heaven.'[14] Huxley's conscious aim in his later works was not to explain why this could be so, but simply to bring people to the point where they were prepared to see the infinite possibilities inexplicably open to them. If he failed to do this, it was not because his views were insincerely held. It was rather that his peculiar gifts as a writer, allied with the obsession with mental and physical suffering that goes right back to the events of his adolescence and early manhood, led him to emphasize those aspects of human behaviour and experience which most contradict the underlying optimism of *The Perennial Philosophy*. Just as he had put all the most unpleasant features of his personality into the character of Anthony Beavis, leaving his charm, tolerance and reliability for his own personal relationships, so he was to continue, in the novels which pursued the examination of mysticism begun in *Eyeless in Gaza*, to make such extensive use of the blackest part of his mind that they quite contradicted the message of hope implicit in his mysticism.

7 Mysticism and the novel

It is indeed as parables exemplifying the formal conclusions of *The Perennial Philosophy* that Huxley's next two novels, *After Many a Summer* (1939) and *Time Must Have a Stop* (1945), are, initially at least, best studied. In both of them, there is a chorus figure whose ideas and presence provide an alternative to the obvious follies which the main narrative depicts; while a well-told tale, and some vividly depicted villains, drive home the moral which is never far below the surface. However apparently scandalous their subject-matter, all the books which Huxley wrote after 1936 were very much in the Arnold tradition of using literature to convey moral truths and the later part of his career could in many ways be seen as the gradual assertion, in his personality as a writer, of the Arnold concern for moral and spiritual values over the iconoclasm and scientific approach of the Huxleys.

It is also noticeable that these two later novels have a much stronger story line than Huxley's earlier fiction. When only ideas matter, and where the characters are cut off from the real world in the country house-party atmosphere of *Crome Yellow* or *Those Barren Leaves*, the narrative does not really count; and a well-made plot would imply that both society itself and the social behaviour of human beings deserve to be taken seriously. Yet while the greater attention given to story-telling in *After Many a Summer* and *Time Must Have a Stop* reflects Huxley's greater concern for moral values, it is still – as it was in the twenties – the more scandalous events that make the novels so immediately readable. And however intellectually vulnerable Huxley's newly propounded religious views may have appeared to certain readers, they destroyed nothing of the appeal which his novels made to the adolescent with an equal interest in sex and ideas. Indeed, the very fact that his mysticism did give rise to argument only increased the appeal of his novels; while the absurd exaggerations of his later fiction, the obvious villains, the sometimes preposterous but always brilliantly expressed ideas, the easily assimilated rival philosophies, the vast historical generalizations, the continuous scorn poured on middle-aged fathers and conventional politicians, the gothic horror of the plots, the combination of Voltairean wit and Bunyanesque religious fervour, all seem in retrospect to have been deliberately calculated to make the same impact on those who were in their teens in the nineteen-forties that *Antic Hay* or *Point Counter Point* had made on similar minds fifteen years earlier. Both *After Many a Summer* and *Time Must Have a*

Stop also deal, albeit superficially, with politics; and both reflect the conclusion, easily accepted in the nineteen-forties, that the industrialized Western democracies offered no hope at all for the future of mankind.

After Many a Summer was the first of Huxley's novels to be set mainly in the United States, and its account of at least one aspect of American life shows Huxley in what was, for him, the rather unusual role of a pioneer whose most fruitful experiments were more successfully exploited by other people. Jo Stoyte, the millionaire whose terror of death provides the mainspring of the plot, has among his many investments The Beverly Pantheon, the 'Personality Cemetery', whose Tower of Resurrection cost two hundred thousand dollars, and whose fountains, statues, perpetual Wurlitzers, Pets' Corner, Church of the Poet and 'Children's Corner with its statues of Peter Pan and the Infant Jesus' are a prefiguration of the comparable horrors which Evelyn Waugh's *The Loved One* did not reveal to most English readers until 1953. Huxley had been living in southern California since 1937, and the impact which a civilization whose advertisement hoardings conspire to offer spiritual healing, colonic irrigation, blocklong hotdogs and 'abiding youth with thrillform brassières', made on his still essentially Victorian personality is presented through the reactions of one of his best observed minor characters, Jeremy Pordage. Jeremy, whose 'small, fluty voice, suggestive of evensong in an English cathedral', is 'a product of Trinity College, Cambridge, ten years before the war' – just as Huxley's Balliol accent was still, as he recognized in 1949, that of 'the Oxford of Jowett and Lewis Carroll' – has been hired by Jo Stoyte to catalogue one of his latest cultural acquisitions, the Hauberk papers. It is Jeremy's discovery of the diary kept by the Fifth Earl, in the late eighteenth century, which brings the action of the novel suddenly back to England, and gives *After Many a Summer* the most outlandishly gruesome ending in all Huxley's fiction.

Jo Stoyte's terror of death, originally created by the text which his maternal grandmother, a Plymouth Sister, had hung over his bed – 'It is a terrible thing to fall into the hands of a living God' – has led him to engage as house physician an expert in longevity with the almost palindromic name of Obispo. At the same time, Jo Stoyte is indulging in what the Fifth Earl refers to as King David's remedy,[1] and it is his affair with the ironically named Virginia Maunciple which leads *After Many a Summer* to become as violent a novel as *Point Counter Point*. Virginia has been seduced by Sigmund Obispo – who perhaps owes his first name less to Huxley's anti-semitism than to his dislike of Freud – and Jo Stoyte finds the two lovers together. Uncharacteristically, however, he is not carrying his automatic pistol, and has to dash to his study to find it. By the time he comes back, Virginia is no longer with Dr Obispo but with his amiable research assistant Pete, whose idealized and wholly innocent love for Virginia has led him to comfort her by placing his hand on her shoulder. Pete is consequently shot in place of the real culprit, and Mr Stoyte is totally in Dr Obispo's power. Only Obispo can sign the death certificate camouflaging the murder into an accident, and his price for doing it is high. The crisis also leads Mr Stoyte to look more favourably at the suggestion which has come to Dr Obispo as a result of Jeremy's continued exploration of the Fifth Earl's diary, and to consider a different remedy against death and old age. The Fifth Earl, it emerges, also had an interest in longevity, and spent much time meditating on the immense age of carps swimming in his ponds. A diet of 'raw, triturated Viscera of freshly opened Carp' restores his youthful vigour to the point where he fathers three illegitimate children at the age of eighty-one, and is subsequently involved in so dramatic a scandal that he has to retire from the world. He does so by arranging a fake funeral, and seeking refuge – now at the age of almost a hundred – in the cellars of his country mansion. Intrigued by this cessation of the diary, Obispo, Stoyte, Jeremy and Virginia take ship to England. There, they find the Fifth Earl, together with the mistress he had persuaded to share in his experiments, still alive at the age of two hundred and one. Unfortunately, however, he has turned into an ape. A dog, someone remarks earlier in the novel, is a wolf that has not fully developed. So, Dr Obispo discovers, man is 'a foetal ape that has not had time to grow up'.[2] Except, of course, for the Fifth Earl. As Jo Stoyte watches the simian quarrellings and copulations with which the Fifth Earl and his mistress fill their eternal life, he breaks the silence:

'How long do you figure it would take before a person went like that?' he said in a slow, hesitating voice. 'I mean, it wouldn't happen at once . . . there'd be a long time while a person . . . well, you know; while he wouldn't change any. And once you get over the first shock – well, they look like they were having a pretty good time. I mean in their own way, of course. Don't you think so, Obispo?' he insisted.

Dr Obispo went on looking at him in silence; then threw back his head and started to laugh again.

Scientifically, the ending of *After Many a Summer* is nonsense. A million years of evolution cannot be reversed in the space of a hundred years, and the grotesque horror of the ending is meaningful only on a moral plane. If men seek to fly above the human condition, they will sink infinitely below it; and the fate of the Fifth Earl bears out the Greek idea that nemesis follows hubris as the night the day. But this is not the only idea in *After Many a Summer*. The chorus figure, Mr Propter, waxes eloquent on what he himself refers to as

the 'old, boring inescapable truths' of the misery of life at a human
level and the possibilities of mystical experience, on the inadequacy
of literature, the case for pacifism, on the advantages of Jeffersonian
democracy, with its cult of economic self-reliance, over modern,
centralized industry, and on the nature of God and the need for a
'calculus of eternity' to transcend the limitations of ordinary language. However, just as Pete is beginning to see that only Mr Propter
can make sense of the 'absurd, insane, diabolical confusion of it all',
he is shot dead by Mr Stoyte; and in the same way that Maurice
Spandrell's deliberate cult of evil has a far deeper effect than the
more attractive theories of Mark Rampion on the way people
behave in *Point Counter Point*, so the Fifth Earl's diary sets out a
view of life which is much more in keeping with Huxley's account
of what life is like than any idea expressed by Mr Propter.

> 'The Christians' writes the Fifth Earl in 1833, 'talk much of Pain,
> but nothing of what they say is to the point. For the most remark-
> able Characteristics of Pain are these: the Disproportion between
> the enormity of physical suffering and its often trifling causes; and
> the manner in which, by annihilating every faculty and reducing
> the body to helplessness, it defeats the Object for which it was
> apparently devised by Nature: viz. to warn the sufferer of the
> approach of danger, whether from within or without. In relation
> to Pain, that empty word, Infinity, comes near to having a
> meaning.'[3]

The Spandrell who considered that this world might be another
planet's hell could only agree, and it is perhaps significant, from a
biographical as well as a literary point of view, that these considerations should be put forward in the assumed voice of an eccentric
eighteenth-century aristocrat. Stylistically, the best passages in *Those
Barren Leaves* were the extracts from Francis Chelliffer's diary in
which Huxley assumes the *persona* of a literary intellectual deliberately seeking self-stultification, and he is just as successful in repro-
ducing the tone of eighteenth-century English in the passages from
the Fifth Earl's diary in *After Many a Summer*. When the Fifth Earl
dines with the Bishop of Winchester and finds his 'claret poor, his
port execrable and his intellectual powers beneath contempt', he
moves into a totally different class from the Mr Propter whose
sermons lack any stylistic qualities whatsoever, and there may well
be a link between the vividness of the Fifth Earl's language and the
unavowed sympathy which part of Huxley's personality felt for his
ideas. Huxley's official belief in the 'fundamental all-rightness of the
world' would normally require him to dismiss the views of the Fifth
Early as nonsense. He is nevertheless unable, as an artist and stylist,
to bring into *After Many a Summer* any character who can serve as

a convincing counterweight to him. Indeed, in so far as the presiding genius in the plot of the novel is the Marquis de Sade, a thinker for whom the Fifth Earl has considerable sympathy and admiration, everything that happens in *After Many a Summer* is a refutation of the metaphysical optimism lying behind Mr Propter's views.

It is curious, in this respect, that Huxley's interest in the Marquis de Sade should be associated with one of the very few errors of fact easily detectable in his books. Going through the Fifth Earl's papers, Jeremy discovers 'bound like a prayer book' a copy of 'that rarest of all works of the Divine Marquis, *Les Cent-Vingt Jours de Sodome*'. However much in character the possession of such a book might have been, it was not a historical possibility. The work was indeed completed as early as 1785, when de Sade succeeded in tabulating, 'on a roll of paper about thirteen yards long and not quite five inches wide', a description of all the known sexual perversions. But the manuscript was lost, and remained a legend until its discovery and publication by Eugene Dhüren in 1904, by which time the Fifth Earl was safely ensconced in his cellars.[4] It is nevertheless de Sade's ideas which inspire not only the conduct and philosophy of the Fifth Earl but also the sexual technique whereby Dr Obispo, as he smugly tells himself, reduces Virginia to 'a mere epileptic body, moaning and gibbering under the excruciations of a pleasure of which you, the Claude Bernard of the subject, were responsible, and of which you remained the enjoying, but always detached, always ironically amused spectator'. Man's body is vulnerable, and his desire for power infinite. Knowledge is power, and the consciousness of power nowhere more intense than in the sexual act. When Dr Obispo 'engineers' Virginia into 'an erotic epilepsy more excruciatingly intense than anything she had known before or imagined possible', he is acting as a scientist, 'wantonly committing enormities' – the phrase is from a definition of science by one of the characters in *Time Must Have a Stop* – in order to show his power. In the book that may have influenced Huxley when he was writing *Brave New World*, Bertrand Russell argued that sadism, in a world wholly dominated by science, would be 'given full range in scientific experiments'.[5] In *After Many a Summer*, Russell's prediction seems to have come true earlier than he anticipated, and the Marquis de Sade to have had a clearer understanding of human nature than any of the thinkers anthologized in *The Perennial Philosophy*.

The fact that it is Jeremy Pordage's scholarship which, albeit unintentionally, places the copy of the *Cent–Vingt Jours* in Dr Obispo's hands is an ironic commentary on the only kind of marriage which Huxley the imaginative writer, as distinct from Huxley the essayist, considered possible between the arts and sciences. And in the world of *After Many a Summer* neither business nor politics gives any more reason for hope than science or scholarship. The Fifth

Earl makes his money out of the slave trade and the enclosure of 'three thousand of acres of common land near Nottingham'; while Jo Stoyte proves himself a worthy modern counterpart by supplementing the fortune already coming in from his oil wells and cemetery by some shrewd but dishonest purchase of land needed for public immigration schemes. The ideals which lead Pete to fight on the Republican side in the Spanish civil war are dismissed by Mr Propter himself as nothing more than 'projections of the ego'; while the political activities of the Western democracies are represented by Jeremy Pordage's brother Tom, 'now back, more or less for good, in the Foreign Office, climbing slowly up the hierarchy, towards posts of greater responsibility and tasks of increasing turpitude'. In this respect, it is not only de Sade's sexual philosophy that Huxley is adapting to the modern world. It is his total disbelief in the possibility of any human being acting virtuously in any social, financial, private or political context.

In so far as it illustrates the supposedly more optimistic views about man's nature and destiny implied by Huxley's mysticism, *After Many a Summer* is consequently not a success. Just as the plot of *Point Counter Point*, with the consistent triumph of Maurice Spandrell, contradicted the humanism of *Do What You Will*, so the portrait of humanity in *After Many a Summer* makes it very difficult to believe in 'the existence, at the very heart of things, of a divine serenity and goodwill' of which Huxley spoke in *The Perennial Philosophy*.

> 'God needs no christening,'
> Pantheist mutters
> 'Love opens shutters
> On heaven's glistening,
> Flesh, key-hole listening,
> Hear what God utters'
> Yes, but God stutters.

wrote the more blatantly cynical Huxley in 1916, and the lines are still peculiarly apt as a description of his own version of 'the hidden God'.[6] Apart from Mr Propter, none of the characters gives any sign at all of benefiting in any way from the existence of God, who for all practical purposes might just as well not exist; and however successfully Mr Propter himself may have contracted out of society by cultivating his own plot of land and even obtaining his own electricity by an ingenious device for storing solar energy, he remains a chorus figure who, like Mark Rampion, has no influence on what happens. This was undoubtedly how Huxley saw himself in 1939: a disillusioned sage, keeping alive the mystical tradition in the hope that some men, in the future, might follow his example and realize

that the only part of the world we can meaningfully improve is ourselves. It is, in a way, a counsel of despair, as well as the attempt to
prove, by one of its most distinguished members, that the English
intellectual upper middle class must now totally abandon any hope
of influencing public behaviour.

ii

Time Must Have a Stop is a less violently pessimistic book than
After Many a Summer, and was the novel which Maria Huxley most
preferred out of all her husband's works.[7] It too has a mystic as
chorus figure, but Bruno Rontini has an immense superiority over
Mr Propter in that he eschews sermons. He also actually succeeds
in doing something to help other people, for it is his intervention at
a crucial moment in the plot that saves an innocent person from
the wholly unintentional but nevertheless highly unpleasant consequences of someone else's selfishness. Sebastian Barnack, a young
and very gifted poet, has been invited by his rich uncle Eustace to
spend a fortnight with him in Florence. Eustace, who had succeeded
where the Tom Cardan of *Those Barren Leaves* had failed and
married a wealthy widow, delights in spending money on art. On the
day of Sebastian's arrival, he buys from an art dealer called Gabriel
Weyl – 'Where every prospect pleases', he is wont to hum as he
goes into his shop, 'And only man is Weyl, *Frères*, Paris, Bruxelles
and Florence' – a pair of magnificent Degas sketches. One of these
inspires Sebastian to write a brief poem to the effect that

> To make a picture others need
> All Ovid and the Nicene creed
> Degas succeeds with one tin tub
> Two buttocks and a pendulous bub

and the quatrain so delights Eustace that he gives his nephew one
of the Degas drawings as a present. He also promises to buy
Sebastian the dinner-jacket which Sebastian's self-righteous father
has refused him, but dies of a heart attack before he can either put
this promise into effect or make public the gift of the Degas.
Sebastian, less deeply affected than he knows he ought to be by his
uncle's sudden death, sells the Degas back to Weyl, only to find that
Eustace's executors notice it is missing. Suspicion falls on a young
Italian servant girl, and Sebastian turns to Bruno Rontini for help.
Bruno persuades Weyl to give him back the picture, so that both
Sebastian and the girl are saved. But as a result of this intervention,
he himself is arrested by Mussolini's police force. Weyl, furious at
having to give up what he had come to regard as his own property,
has denounced Bruno for having contacts with anti-fascist political

agents; and Sebastian has provided a pretext for this accusation by boasting casually, to Weyl, of his father's association with a well-known Italian liberal politician.[8]

This apparent defeat of virtue by a cruel and violent world is not, however, merely a reversion to the dominant pattern in Huxley's early novels, where the spirit is invariably defeated by the flesh. The example of Bruno's unselfishness leave such a mark on Sebastian that we find him, in the epilogue to the novel, in 1944, converted to the same mystical philosophy that had inspired Bruno's life. Like *Eyeless in Gaza*, *Time Must Have a Stop* is the novel of a conversion, but Bruno Rontini is a more attractive saint than James Miller, and Sebastian Barnack a less consistently caddish hero than Anthony Beavis. The intellectual energy which threatened to burst open the seams of *Eyeless in Gaza* has settled down to a steady and less strident conviction that one particular way of thought is undoubtedly superior to all others, and it is perhaps for this reason that the novel ends with a serenity which explains Maria Huxley's preference. There are, however, other reasons for considering *Time Must Have a Stop* the most intriguing as well as the most challenging of Huxley's 'mystical' novels, and for explaining why Huxley himself preferred it to his other fiction.[9]

Paradoxically, the first of these reasons begins by having nothing to do with mysticism. It is the presence of Uncle Eustace, a character who has stepped straight out of the novels which Huxley wrote in the twenties, the period in which the main action of the novel is set. He is the Mr Keith of Norman Douglas's *South Wind*, translated only a little farther north, to Florence, and only slightly altered by his successive incarnations as the Mr Scogan of *Crome Yellow* or the Tom Cardan of *Those Barren Leaves*. It is perhaps natural, in the circumstances, that he should make so immediate an appeal to Sebastian. His rejection of the hard, puritanical idealism of Sebastian's father, his apology for hedonism, his sympathy for the 'idlers and wasters' who 'demonstrably do less mischief than the other fellows', his tolerance, his wit, his knowledge of art, are all calculated to appeal to adolescents, and the effect he has on Sebastian is in this respect an epitome of the attraction which Huxley's early novels exercised over their readers when they were first published. Uncle Eustace is not, however, made to be quite so sensible about food as he is about ideas. After a night's sleep induced by a pint of stout and a plate of anchovy sandwiches, he breakfasts off porridge, two poached eggs, toast, kippers, scones and marmalade; has *lasagne verdi*, chianti and creamed breasts of turkey for lunch; champagne, two portions of creamed fish, creamed – *sic* – breasts of chicken and chocolate soufflé with cream for dinner; two glasses of brandy with his cigar; and – not surprisingly – dies of a heart attack the same evening. One can accept Philip Quarles, in *Point Counter Point*, drinking claret with his fish because he is, after all, Huxley himself; and Huxley once tried to live exclusively off beans.[10] But although a novelist who makes a professional gourmet disgrace himself like this would normally forfeit the reader's credulity as well as his sympathy, Uncle Eustace tends at first sight rather to benefit from Huxley's obvious animus against him. Indeed, this sympathy lingers for quite a long time, and threatens to upset the whole moral balance of the book. It is only in the context of Huxley's major technical experiment in *Time Must Have a Stop*, the attempt to depict life after death in the light of the teachings advanced in *The Tibetan Book of the Dead*, that the character of Eustace Barnack begins to reveal its limitations.

An ambition to illustrate certain moral concepts by providing an imaginative description of life after death inspired at least two other books published at about the same time as Huxley's *Time Must Have a Stop*: Jean-Paul Sartre's *Huis Clos* and C. S. Lewis's *The Great Divorce*. All three authors, however great their ideological differences, also reveal the same automatic dismissal of the traditional belief in an Avenging Deity actively punishing sinners in hell. Instead, each insists on the idea that we are punished in the next world solely by what we have allowed ourselves to become in this one, and just as Lewis's Napoleon shuts himself away from God by building immense replicas of Empire palaces, so Huxley's Uncle Eustace deliberately closes his eyes to the Clear Light of the Void. And just as Sartre's coward, in *Huis Clos*, has the chance to walk away from his tormentors and thus prove his claim to be a brave man by trying something different, so Eustace Barnack remains free, if he so wishes, to turn away from his ordinary self and accept the salvation offered to him. If he does not do so, it is because he chooses to remain a particular kind of person, one whose gluttony is an integral part of the lack of will-power which now keeps him in this self-inflicted hell.

Unlike *The Great Divorce* or *Huis Clos*, the section of *Time Must Have a Stop* which attempts to describe Eustace's experiences after death has sometimes been regarded as difficult to understand, and even so perceptive a critic as Peter Bowering writes that this part of the novel can be 'almost meaningless without a prior reading of *The Tibetan Book of the Dead*'.[11] This is not really so, and although it is an interesting scholarly exercise to see how Huxley has in fact based his descriptions on the recommendations to the dying contained in this particular version of Buddhism, the passages are fully comprehensible without this knowledge. Eustace dies, and immediately a light begins to shine, to welcome him into an eternity of bliss if he will only agree to let go of his separate self and merge himself in it. Eustace refuses, and is encouraged to cling on to his independent existence by a spiritualist *séance* held in his own Florentine villa. This enables him to taste, through the medium, the 'mingled savours of garlic and chocolate, red wine and – yes – kidneys – haunting the tongue and palate', all the earthly sensations he has so much enjoyed and which offer a more comfortable paradise than the 'blue, shining stillness'. This stillness, 'delicate, unutterably beautiful like the essence of all skies and flowers, like the silent principle and potentiality of all music' appeals to him in vain, and he eventually chooses to be reincarnated in the child already conceived by Gabriel Weyl and his wife. Indeed, so great is his appetite for immediate physical existence that he makes this choice in spite of the foreknowledge which he has that this child, a Jew, will suffer the agony of seeing its mother killed during the invasion of France in 1940.[12] In *The Perennial Philosophy* Huxley quotes a passage from *The Tibetan Book of the Dead* describing the *Bardo* state, the 'intermediate state' immediately following death, as one in which 'the soul is judged – or rather judges itself by choosing, in accord with the character forged during its life on earth, what sort of after-life it shall have'. *Time Must Have a Stop* quite clearly shows Eustace doing this, and thus illustrates both the remark in *The Perennial Philosophy* that most suffering is self-inflicted, and Huxley's more unexpected belief in the doctrine of reincarnation.

Perhaps for this very reason, the novel does not remove any of the objections which can be put forward, either on intellectual or on ethical grounds, to the views expressed in *The Perennial Philosophy*. In so far as it involves a belief both in some kind of life after death and in the possibility of reincarnation, it clearly goes against Huxley's rejection of metaphysics; and in so far as Eustace is seen suffering the torments of the damned because he remains attached to the pleasures of the table and the delights of occasionally unorthodox sex, it once again raises the question of whether Huxley's mystical views are in any way meaningful on a human level. If a kindly uncle, who has harmed nobody and helped whomsoever he could, is placed so firmly in a self-inflicted hell, what torments are left for Hitler? And if it is true, as the Sebastian of *Time Must Have a Stop* eventually argues, that the normal human virtues of courage, reliability, and unselfishness are what lead society to catastrophic acts of self-destruction, then how can we formulate any kind of rational ethic? All acts other than those inspired by the total detachment of the mystic are equally wrong; and there is no means of distinguishing between Stalin and Lord Attlee, between Camus and the Marquis de Sade, or between the World Health Organization and the OGPU. If we are doomed to the torments of another life and the agony of perpetual reincarnation because we enjoy food, love our children, serve our country, or grieve over the death of our friends, then we do indeed seem to be the victims of a vast and cruel practical joke.

All the higher religions do, of course, insist on the unpalatable facts that many are called but few are chosen, that only he who would lose his life shall save it, that Christ came to bring not peace but a sword, and that God should never be judged by the purely human conceptions of right and wrong which man has evolved for his social convenience. In this respect, especially in this ecumenical age, the more pessimistic side of Huxley's mysticism can have the same salutary effect on discussions of mysticism that the teachings of the existentialists have on more orthodox faiths. Religion and humanism cannot be reconciled, and Kierkegaard is right when he insists upon the unbridgeable gulf separating God from man. The implications of Uncle Eustace's 'Bardo' state are fundamentally no different from those of Matthew X, 35, and XIX, 29. The task of reminding the laxer Pelagians of the true implications of their official faith was one for which Huxley was in many ways peculiarly suited – perhaps better suited, in fact, than he was to writing novels. Yet curiously enough, neither *Time Must Have a Stop* nor *After Many a Summer* is as utterly depressing, even to the unregenerate reader, as the philosophy underlying them might suggest. This is partly because Huxley's pessimism tends to backfire so that the very intensity of his gloom provides a springboard for a return to cheerfulness based on the reflection that we can't possibly all be as bad as that. More particularly, however, precisely because he is a novelist, Huxley's teaching is put forward through the medium of certain characters. And, as happens with other, greater writers, these characters themselves often seem to take charge of the book, and to acquire a life and independence which Huxley's formal views would theoretically deny them.

This is as true of Sebastian Barnack, with his poetry and sexual obsessions, as it is of Uncle Eustace and his wholly earthy, cynical wisdom. In the case of the first, one ought to feel repelled, and in a way Huxley is repelled, by the sub-plot which develops in partial counter-point to Eustace's death. For Sebastian is seduced by one of the guests at Eustace's Florentine Villa, an attractive twenty-four-year-old widow called Veronica Thwale, who uses him to be 'scientific to the point of enormity' by going to bed with him on the very night after she has agreed to marry her second husband. Casual references to the charm of birching place the affair on the same rather odd sexual plane as the preoccupations of Dr Obispo and the Fifth Earl, and Huxley's interest in the seamier side of sex seems to increase rather than diminish as his official world view becomes more and more puritanical. Yet the phrase describing Veronica's 'despairing insatiability' contains more than a hint of genuine sympathy for those who can neither be happy on human terms nor receive any help from the mystical tradition, and this may well have been another factor in the preference which Huxley's first wife expressed for *Time Must Have a Stop*. The phrase *era tanto buono*, so frequently applied to Huxley himself by his Italian housekeeper, is also used by Eustace's servants to describe their master at the very moment when the 'clear light of the void' is urging him to abandon the human characteristics which once made him so attractive.

8 Essays, self-portraits and history

It could be argued that *Time Must Have a Stop* is Huxley's last major attempt to use fiction as a medium for expressing his ideas. Only one of the books he published after 1945, *The Genius and the Goddess* in 1955, sets out to tell a story in a conventionally realistic setting, and even this is more of a long short story than an orthodox novel. As Geoffrey Gorer has shown, *Island* (1963) is more an anthropologist's report on an imaginary paradise than a study of how human beings actually behave in society, while *Ape and Essence* (1946), a vision of the future even more depressing than *Brave New World*, is actually presented as a film-script. It is not difficult to find reasons for this move away from the novel. Huxley described himself on several occasions as an essayist who happened to write novels, and the essay element is very visible in several of his books. He received, as he said in one interview, no help at all from his subconscious when elaborating his plots, and though the recurrence of certain sexual themes might lead a Freudian to take this statement with a pinch of salt, it is certainly true that his narrative is often only a pretext for the literary, philosophical and political digressions in which he is clearly most interested. As Philip Quarles comments somewhat ruefully in *Point Counter Point*, the chief defect of the novel of ideas is that 'you must write about people who have ideas to express – which excludes all but 0.01 per cent of the human race', and Huxley certainly knew that his novels gave an inadequate account of ordinary human experience. It may well be that he considered *Time Must Have a Stop* to have been his most successful novel because he had, in his description of Uncle Eustace's 'Bardo' state, actually shown an intellectual experiencing reality instead of just talking about it.

A move away from the novel did not, of course, involve a new departure in Huxley's work. He had always written essays, and collections such as *Music at Night* (1931), *The Olive Tree* (1932) or *Adonis and the Alphabet* (1956) are among his most aesthetically satisfying books. Neither are such collections irrelevant either to the successive self-portraits presented by his fiction or to the different ideas on which he tried to base his various novels. Thus his essay on Tibet, published in *On the Margin* in 1923, not only anticipates the general iconoclasm of *Do What You Will*. Its ironic comment that 'the spectacle of an ancient and elaborate civilization of which no detail is not entirely idiotic is in the highest degree comforting and

G

refreshing' is yet another indication of how radically his views were to change later in his career when he used the *Tibetan Book of the Dead* to express a major theme in *Time Must Have a Stop*. The same element of intellectual autobiography is also present in *Along the Road* (1925), where his analysis of 'the best picture' – Piero della Francesca's *Resurrection* – emphasizes his liking for 'natural, spontaneous and unpretentious grandeur', and desire to worship 'what is admirable in man'. The link here is with the humanism of *Do What You Will*, while his remark in the same volume that he would personally 'sooner be Faraday than Shakespeare' because 'the artist . . . must fatally pass much of his life in the emotional world of human contacts' again indicates how much of himself Huxley did put into the character of Philip Quarles in *Point Counter Point*.[1]

T. H. Huxley as a Man of Letters, on the other hand, originally given as the *Huxley Memorial Lecture* in May 1932, is less informative biographically than one might perhaps expect. It is primarily an analysis of his grandfather's literary style, and becomes relevant to Huxley's own work only at one point. 'Pain and sorrow knock at our doors more loudly than pleasure and happiness; and the prints of their footsteps are less easily effaced' is a remark which he quotes primarily to illustrate his grandfather's predilection for the *caesura* sentence; and here as elsewhere, this lecture gives most tempting encouragement to writers with a fondness for semicolons.[2] But the very restraint with which T. H. Huxley expresses himself underlines by contrast the almost hysterical note which the same idea assumes in *After Many a Summer*, and epitomizes the difference between the two most famous members of the Huxley family. In Thomas Henry, the metaphysical pessimism underlying his work was kept in check by his six children as well as by his active involvement in the evolving science and stable society of his day; whereas in the case of his grandson, this pessimism was given freer rein as much through the isolation that was Huxley's lot as a writer as by the disintegration of his own and his grandfather's world.

Although the essay on the French philosopher Maine de Biran, published in *Themes and Variations* in 1950, deals primarily with mysticism and the methods of analysis elaborated in the nineteen-thirties by the American physiologist W. H. Sheldon, it has even greater interest as a partly involuntary self-portrait. For Sheldon, human beings could be analysed in terms of three basic components: endomorphy, associated with fatness, extraversion and a cheerful gregariousness; mesomorphy, with a muscular physique, large bones, aggressiveness and a 'lust for power'; and ectomorphy, with small bones, a slender build, stringy muscles, and an intense interest in the things of the mind. The three corresponding psychological types are viscerotonics – Pickwick, Uncle Eustace, Falstaff, G. K. Chesterton; somatotonics – Hotspur, Sebastian Barnack's father, Ian Paisley,

Bulldog Drummond, the Roderick Spode of *The Code of the Woosters*; and cerebretonics – Hamlet, Ivan Karamazov, Voltaire, Shelley and Huxley himself. Obviously, Sheldon insists, most people are a mixture of all three types, and probably the best example of this mixture in literature is Dmitri Karamazov, whose viscerotonic appetite for sheer physical life goes hand in hand both with the violent, somatotonic temperament which he inherits from his father, and with the speculative tendencies more highly developed in his two cerebretonic brothers. Huxley himself was an extreme example of the cerebretonic – in 1943 he described both himself and his son Matthew as 'lanky ectomorphs'; and commented in 1945 that 'the hypersensitiveness of neurotic cerebretonics can often be cured (i.e. masked) by the simple procedure of feeding them a diet rich in cream and bananas'[3] – and it is clear from his treatment of Maine de Biran that much of the interest which this philosopher had for him stemmed from the fact that he too fell so neatly into this Sheldonian category. So, in fact, do all the autobiographical characters in Huxley's novels – Philip Quarles, Bernard Marx, Anthony Beavis, Sebastian Barnack – and the essay on Maine de Biran is a further summary of how Huxley tended, perhaps unjustly, to see himself: inapt and inept in personal relationships, excessively retiring and unaggressive, unduly subject to the whims of his body, an extreme cerebretonic whose relative inefficiency in the ordinary affairs of life was counter-balanced by his capacity for abstract thought. One could indeed argue that it was because he himself fitted so well into this frame-work that Huxley adopted so relatively uncritical an attitude towards the Sheldonian hypothesis. For it is fairly obvious, even to a layman, that neither Hitler, Napoleon nor Sir Winston Churchill were markedly somatotonic types, and Soljenitsin noted in *The First Circle* that Stalin was not a large man.[4]

Another of Huxley's hobby horses, vegetarianism, also shows itself in the Maine de Biran essay, when he comments on the Christian habit of referring to priests and rulers as shepherds. This analogy, he claims, 'was first used by the herd-owning, land-destroying, meat-eating and war-waging peoples who replaced the horticulturalists of the first civilization and put an end to the Golden Age of Peace, which not long since was regarded as a mere myth, but is now revealed by the light of archaeology as a proto- and pre-historical reality'; and it is clear from this Rousseau-istic com-ment that Huxley's essays frequently reflect both the didactic tones and the liking for unconventional ideas which first made itself heard in *Eyeless in Gaza* and *Ends and Means*.

What is perhaps most noticeable about Huxley's later career as an essayist is the gradual disappearance of purely literary topics. Although Huxley still regarded himself, as late as 1958, as sufficiently a man of letters to remark, when a Brazilian newspaper gave a daily outline of his views under the heading *O Sabio*, 'It is the only place in the world where anyone wants to read a literary gent's opinions about things in general day after day',[5] his own interests had turned several years previously to historical, social and political matters. Huxley's best essays on literature all come before the major turning point of 1936, and two of them, *Tragedy and the Whole Truth* and *Vulgarity in Literature*, date from 1931 and 1930 respectively. The first, with its thesis that tragedy is 'chemically pure' art, life with all the irrelevancies taken out, is a fascinating gloss both on the Shakespeare whom Huxley liked and the Racine whom he didn't, while at the same time a deliberate comment on the kind of books he personally was trying to write. Thus when Mark Staithes, in *Eyeless in Gaza*, 'complained of the profound untruthfulness of even the best imaginative literature' and 'began to catalogue its omissions', he is certainly echoing Huxley's own views. What he deplores is the 'almost total neglect of those small, physiological events that decide whether day-to-day living shall have a pleasant or an unpleasant tone. Excretion, for example, with its power to make or mar the day. Digestion. And, for the heroines of novel and drama, menstruation.' From this point of view, Huxley is infinitely more truthful a writer than the Flaubert whose Emma Bovary spends seven hours with her lover in a cab, and even the most unpleasant incidents in *Eyeless in Gaza* – Helen's abortion, the amputation of Mark Staithes's leg – can be seen as part of a consistent attempt to tell the truth about human existence. Yet while this aspect of his work still makes him very up to date in 1972, it is also linked with another feature of his novels on which he himself, less consciously this time, has also commented in one of his best known literary essays, *Vulgarity in Literature*.

Thus Huxley is a writer who consistently emphasizes the extremes in human life – of intellectuality, of pointlessness, of physiological irrelevance (little Phil needing to go to the lavatory when waiting for his parents to come back from abroad; Sebastian Barnack masturbating in a hot bath while his uncle dies of a heart attack), of spiritual ecstacy and physical disgust – and there is a curious relationship in this respect between *Vulgarity in Literature* and some of his own books. It is not that he is vulgar in the true sense of the word, which he rightly diagnoses as being pretentious. He is not like the Edgar Allan Poe whose over-poetical rhymes and rhythms he compares to a *parvenu* 'wearing a diamond ring on every finger', and whose 'finer shades of vulgarity' remained hidden to foreign observers such as Baudelaire, Mallarmé and Valéry. It is rather that he never developed the aristocratic skill of being ordinary enough to disarm admiration, the gentlemanly habit of limiting his knowledge, as his brother Julian once suggested to him he should, to 'what the company needed', the art of discreetly fusing narrative with ideas to the point where the reader is rather flattered by his own intelligence than overwhelmed by the brilliance of the author. It is not unusual, when discussing Huxley with WEA students, to hear him dismissed as 'a know-all'. Just as ridicule kills in France, such an accusation can spell death in England.[6]

Nowhere, however, was Huxley's breadth of knowledge used to better effect than in his essays on the visual arts, and it is extraordinary that a man who was virtually blind in one eye and had only imperfect vision in the other should have known so much about painting, sculpture and architecture. Yet Huxley not only knew where every picture was in the many galleries he visited, when it was painted and in what historical circumstances. He was also, as Kenneth Clark has observed, 'one of the most discerning lookers of our time', whose ability to give a 'description of the subject of a picture in an artist's own terms' is a most rare gift in literary men. And just as Huxley's knowledge of science or philosophy invariably found its way into his novels, so his appreciation of the visual arts was frequently incorporated – often more successfully – into the patterns of his fiction. In *Antic Hay*, it is the model of Wren's plans for London that serves as a reference point for beauty and sanity in a chaotic world, while in *After Many a Summer* it is a Vermeer portrait of a lady, 'sitting at the very heart of an equation, in a world where beauty and logic, painting and analytical geometry, had become one', which provides both the aptest comment on the fury of Jo Stoyte as he looks ferociously for his gun, and the most attractive alternative to the criminal follies which he represents. It is indeed through his interest in art that Huxley is most successful in amalgamating the two sides of his literary activity, his work as an essayist and the contribution which he makes to the literature of ideas; and *Grey Eminence*, the study he published in 1942 of Father Joseph, Cardinal Richelieu's assistant and principal adviser in home and domestic policy, is a particularly good example of how his two major interests, the aesthetic and the ethical, can be woven together.

ii

A lack of enthusiasm for the artistic style known as the baroque appears early in Huxley's career when he describes the seventeenth century, in *Along the Road* (1925), as the 'age of baroque, of kingly and clerical display' and comments on how grotesque the 'too expressive, theatrical gestures of the baroque architects and decorators' becomes because they are 'trying to express something tragic in terms of a style essentially comic'. Here, however, his distaste is primarily aesthetic, and it is not until *Ends and Means*, in 1937, that he sees the 'hysterical, almost epileptic' violence of what he then calls the emotionality of baroque art in a fuller context. It was, he argues, part of a deliberate attempt, in Catholicism, to replace the more impersonal 'way of knowledge' fully accepted in Eastern religions as a possible means of attaining God by that 'devotion to a personal deity' which, in Huxley's view, had always been one of the worst aspects in the Christian tradition. Neither was the substitution, in baroque art, of intense yearning for quiet contemplation the only reason for Huxley's dislike. 'The throne', he wrote in *Beyond the Mexique Bay*, 'is the natural ally of the altar, and both, for the same ceremonial reasons, have steps.' The Catholic Counter Reformation, which sought to make itself the dominant intellectual influence during the seventeenth century, found a natural ally in the spiritual bullying implicit in the spurious dignity which baroque grandeur gave to kings and priests, and the Huxley who had always felt 'a passion for personal freedom' had political as well as aesthetic reasons for disliking this particular artistic style.[7]

He also had other motives whose apparent irrelevance to the art and politics of the Counter Reformation only underlines the consistency of the philosophy he had elaborated for himself as a result of his conversion to mysticism. Thus in 1956, in *The Education of an Amphibian*, he remarks that the adage 'If you want to see, stop trying', has a wider application than the immediate role which it plays in the Bates system of eye training. Indeed, he continues, this aphorism was invented for the express purpose of allowing the 'deep wisdom of the body' to overcome the bad habits which people had acquired through their conscious efforts, and he remarks in this context that 'left to itself, the physiological intelligence is almost incapable of making a mistake'.[8] This view is fundamental not only to his early agnosticism – the Bull at Benares, in *Jesting Pilate*, behaves sensibly because it follows its instincts, whereas the worshippers on the banks of the Ganges act stupidly as a result of the religious ideas created by their conscious mind – but also to the synthesis which he strove to establish, from the nineteen-thirties onwards, between the study of human physiology and the findings of the mystics. Indeed, in so far as his thesis in *The Doors of Perception*, in 1953, is the Bergsonian one that, by using our conscious, analytical intellect to gain control of the world around us, we have effectively prevented ourselves from seeing what really exists, the mistrust which Huxley shows for the practices of baroque devotion can be linked to his much better known writings on the effects of mescalin. Father Joseph, writes Huxley in *Grey Eminence*, 'never succeeded in overcoming his all too natural desire to take the kingdom of heaven by violence', and the intense intellectuality of seventeenth-century Catholicism tended to hide the Ultimate Reality from him just as effectively as the language which modern man uses to think about the world leads him to mistake his various philosophies for a correct account of existence. Like his contemporaries whose yearnings are reflected in the intense, emotional lines of the ecstatic figures in baroque sculpture, Father Joseph tried too hard to attain that unification with the underlying goodness of the world which, for Huxley, reveals itself in two basic ways: to the natural mystic as a result of a patient 'waiting on God' in the state of physical and psychological relaxation known as meditation; and those who, by a correct use of drugs such as mescalin, so cleanse their doors of perception that everything, in Blake's words, 'appears to them as it is, that is infinite'. Mescalin, in other words, can induce a state of relaxation, of openness to experience, which is precisely the opposite of the tension and conscious striving reflected in baroque art; and in this respect there is a very clear link between Huxley's unfavourable analysis of seventeenth-century Catholicism in *Grey Eminence*, his reading of F. Matthias Alexander, his adoption of the Bates system for eye training, and his defence, in *The Doors of Perception* and *Island*, of the controlled use of certain drugs.

This analysis of Father Joseph's 'frenzy of zeal' is, of course, only one aspect of *Grey Eminence*. In the emphasis which it places upon the relationship between what Father Joseph did and what subsequently happened in Europe, this 'study in religion and politics' is very much the work of a committed historian, closely related to the time at which it was written and specifically aimed at proving certain theses. These are that Father Joseph, who was Cardinal Richelieu's chief political assistant between 1614 and 1638, is indirectly responsible for two of the greatest evils of the present day: nationalist wars and totalitarian government. By advising Richelieu on how best to prolong the Thirty Year War, Father Joseph not only helped to kill one-third of the population of Central Europe. He also created exactly the right conditions for the later domination of Germany by Prussia, and the consequent establishment of the military machine which, in the year when *Grey Eminence* was published, had conquered the mainland of Europe. Moreover, by helping Richelieu to destroy all opposition to the Crown, Father Joseph enabled Louis XIV's 'characteristically totalitarian'[9] ambitions to create, in seventeenth-century France, a state which was prevented only by its own inefficiency from attaining the same degree of spiritual uniformity as Hitler's Germany.

It is rather curious, when one remembers the hostility towards Catholicism which shows itself throughout Huxley's work – especially on the question of birth control – to discover that something very like his thesis on Cardinal Richelieu was put forward in 1931 by the militantly Catholic historian and man of letters, Hilaire Belloc. The parallel is even more surprising when one remembers Huxley's private little dig at Belloc's *Cautionary Tales* in *After Many a Summer* – 'Curious how many English Catholics take to comic versifying', he remarks of Jeremy Pordage's brother Tom, who becomes a convert and 'publishes a volume of comic verse two days

after the sack of Nanking' – and there can be no question of a direct
influence. Both writers nevertheless maintain that the Cardinal's
readiness to ally himself with the German protestants – and even
with the infidel Turks – if this could serve the interests of Catholic
France constitutes an important turning point in modern history,
and both quote the remark which Pope Urban VIII is said to have
made after Richelieu's death: 'If there is a God, then Cardinal
Richelieu has much to answer for; but if there is not, he has done
very well.' There, however, the parallel finishes. Huxley had no
sympathy for the spiritual totalitarianism implied by Belloc's vision
of a Europe united under the Catholic Church and he was, in any
case, essentially concerned less with Richelieu himself than with his
assistant. Indeed, in the first pages of *Grey Eminence*, Father Joseph
almost becomes another of the semi-autobiographical characters on
to whom Huxley projects not only his immediate intellectual preoccupations but also his own private experience of the world. Like
Huxley, Father Joseph was an intellectually precocious child, with
a marked tendency to 'shrink from what he felt to be the indecency
of expressed emotional intimacy with other human beings'. When
he was ten, his father died; and when the first paroxysm of grief was
past, writes Huxley, 'there remained with him, latent at ordinary
times, but always ready to come to the surface, a haunting sense of
the vanity, the transience, the hopeless precariousness of all merely
human happiness'. The parallel with Huxley's reaction to the death
of his mother when he was fourteen is almost uncanny, and the
personal similarity between the two men becomes even more marked
later in the volume. In 1604, at the age of twenty-seven, 'an aggrava-
tion of that progressive defect of vision which advanced throughout
his life until, at the end, he was nearly blind' prevents Father Joseph
from following his intended career as a theologian and man of
learning. Instead, he turns to the world of men, and the biographical
similarity with Huxley's inability, because of his own poor eyesight,
to follow the medical career which he had originally planned, takes
on a more intellectual aspect. Like Huxley, Father Joseph reads
widely in the mystical tradition. In addition to the more orthodox
Christian thinkers, he knew, as Huxley remarks in his casually well
informed manner, 'Dionysius the Areopagite's *Mystical Theology*
and *Divine Names*, the mystical writings of Hugh and Richard of
St. Victor and St. Bernard', as well as 'Ruysbroeck and two lesser
contemplatives of the fifteenth and sixteenth centuries respectively,
Henry de Herp and the Benedictine Abbot, Blosius'.[10] But, unlike
Huxley, he goes into politics, and it is with the incompatibility
between politics and mysticism that *Grey Eminence* is essentially
concerned.

Father Joseph, according to Huxley, 'believed he could live and
work, even at power politics, in a state of "holy indifference" very

similar to the state recommended in the *Bhagavad Gita* to the hero Arjuna as he prepares to go into battle'. But experience proved him to be wrong, and his whole life suffered from the infection given off by his political acts. Yet although God and power politics do not mix, Father Joseph was encouraged to think they might by the very doctrines which, as Huxley argues, are common to both Eastern and Western mysticism. Huxley himself prefaced the new translation of the *Bhagavad Gita* which Christopher Isherwood made in 1948, and certainly knew at the time of writing *Grey Eminence* of the injunction to Arjuna to fight vigorously but 'with detachment'. What he does not seem quite to have realized, before beginning his account of Father Joseph's career, is that this injunction is not so much morally neutral as ethically nihilistic. If one is detached, one doesn't care, and it was precisely Father Joseph's mysticism which enabled him to contribute so effectively to the blindness and insanity of seventeenth-century Europe. 'Few political idealists', writes Huxley, 'have spent half a life-time brooding upon the torture and death of a man-god, by comparison with whose sufferings those of ordinary human beings are so infinitesimal as to be practically negligible';[11] and it requires only the slightest shift of emphasis to show how this indifference towards the fate of people in the world could be fitted into the Eastern view of physical reality as *Maya*, illusion. Since human beings do not really exist, Father Joseph had every licence to use treachery, fraud and violence in the furtherance of the greater glory of France. Nihilism and tyranny, as Camus argued in *L'Homme révolté*, go automatically hand in hand because both refuse to believe in people as individuals.

Huxley naturally tried to answer, in the text itself, the overwhelming case against mysticism unwittingly advanced by the account of Father Joseph's activities in *Grey Eminence*. 'As a matter of historical fact', he observes, 'many of the great theocentrics have been men and women of enormous and beneficent activity', and he links this remark to his own dislike of industrialism and centralization by adding that the work which theocentrics do is 'always marginal' and always directed to units small enough 'to be capable of shared spiritual experience and of moral and rational conduct'.[12] The sympathy which Huxley felt for the Society of Friends is closely linked to this view, and he never ceased to insist that no salvation was attainable to anyone who accepted the norms of our own highly complex technological society. In this context, his final judgment on Father Joseph, like the possibly unconscious emphasis which he gives to the similarities between himself and the subject of his book, also takes on an autobiographical tone. According to the Indian view, he writes, it is 'a fatal thing for the members of one caste to usurp the functions that properly belong to another', and proceeds to comment that Father Joseph is 'an eminent example' of what happens when *brahmins* forsake the meditation which is their natural calling and go in for politics.[13] The place for cerebretonics, Huxley is implying, is essentially in the library. If they are going to come down into the world of men, they must do so only in order to join small groups of like-minded individualists, and must not involve themselves in any of the large-scale activities of the modern world.

As in the social implications of *Brave New World*, this rejection of the traditions of the class into which he was born again marks Huxley out as an exception even within his own family. Neither his brother Julian, who accepted in 1946 the post as first Director General of Unesco, nor his cousin Gervas, who spent the second world war, in the words of *Who's Who*, as 'adviser to the Ministry of Information on publicity to and about the Empire and on relations with the American forces in the United Kingdom', found it necessary to adopt so extreme an attitude, and it is again a curious example of the difference between Huxley the writer and Aldous the man that his private relationships were in no way affected by the views he put forward in his books. According to *Grey Eminence*, anybody who touched pitch would inevitably be defiled; and for a pacifist and advocate of non-attachment, there could surely be nothing blacker than propaganda for the Empire. But in 1948, when Gervas dined with him in New York, Aldous displayed 'a fascinated and wholly objective interest in the art and techniques of advertising, public relations and market research'. It was an attitude which one would have thought, from his books, quite impossible for the man who had such harsh words to say about the not wholly dissimilar work that Jeremy Pordage's brother Tom did in the Foreign Office – 'working away at the precise spot where he could do the maximum amount of harm to the greatest possible number of people'.[14]

iii

Ten years after the publication of *Grey Eminence*, Huxley returned to the century and subject which seem to have had an almost obsessive attraction for him, and wrote the book by which, in 1972, he is probably known to more people than ever read either his essays or his novels. *The Devils of Loudun*, first published in October 1952, is the only one of his novels to have achieved fame by being adapted to the mass media, and there is some irony in the fact that Ken Russell's film *The Devils* will have made more money in a year than Huxley received from his books during his whole lifetime. For all its extravagance, the film is not a wholly inaccurate adaptation. Admittedly, by concentrating on the political aspects of Urbain Grandier's trial for witchcraft in 1634, it reveals how all-pervasive the fashionable anti-authoritarianism of the early nineteen-seventies can be. But Grandier was just as much a victim of the totalitarian ambitions of Cardinal Richelieu as he was the object of vengeance for the private enemies whom his pride had led him to make, and the book has the same implicit defence of the open society as *Grey Eminence*. The physical horror of the scene in which Grandier is burnt at the stake is again no betrayal of the book. 'After all', writes Huxley, quoting Montaigne, 'it is rating one's conjectures at a very high price to roast a man alive on the strength of them'; and the agnosticism underlying all his work is inseparable from his obsession with the physical suffering which men inflict on other men.

In 1952, however, the main subject-matter of the book was more obviously relevant to the immediate political atmosphere of the time, and Huxley was expressing a widespread attitude when he argued that only a relatively narrow gap separated the witch-hunts of the seventeenth century from the excesses of the Cold War. In the very same year that Arthur Miller used the Salem witch trials of 1692 as an allegory to comment on America during the McCarthy era, Huxley was writing in *The Devils of Loudun* that 'the destinies of the world are in the hands of self-made demoniacs, of men who are possessed by, and who manifest, the evil they have chosen to see in others'; while the essence of Jean-Paul Sartre's attack on French anti-communism in the nineteen-forties can be summed up in Huxley's very characteristic remark that 'like the mercurial and antimonial poisonings of earlier years, like the sulpha poisoning and serum-fevers of the present, the Loudun epidemic was an "iatrogenic disease", produced and fostered by the very physicians who were supposed to be restoring the patients to health'.[15] Yet there was, in the nineteen-fifties and sixties, nothing imaginary about the Communists occupying Eastern Europe or threatening West Berlin, and *The Devils of Loudun* shows the same refusal to distinguish between the half loaf of Western democracy and the 'no bread' of totalitarianism which had characterized Huxley's political thinking in the nineteen-thirties.

It is not, however, only a political book, and has other themes which link it more firmly to Huxley's more general philosophy. Thus it is a sustained if sometimes paradoxical defence of his belief in the fundamental goodness of nature – a belief reflected in the nineteen-fifties by his praise for vegetarianism in *Variations on a Philosopher*, but going right back to the nineteen-twenties and his comments on the sacred bull at Benares in *Jesting Pilate* – and the events described in *The Devils of Loudun* come about precisely because men have tried to repress the natural sexual urge by shutting women up in convents and insisting that priests should remain celibate. If Soeur Jeanne des Anges, an 'average sensual woman', had been able to marry and have children, she would never have developed the frustrated passion for Urbain Grandier which led her to accuse him of seeking to possess her soul and body by witchcraft; and had Christian theologians not chosen to regard nature as evil, they would never have developed the elaborate theories which justified burning people at the stake for supposed commerce with the Devil. When, at the very moment that Grandier is burnt alive, a flock of pigeons suddenly swoops down from the sky, the parson's enemies greet them as 'a troop of devils come to fetch away his soul'. More probably, comments Huxley, they are merely 'obeying the laws of their own, their blessedly other-than-human nature' – just as the bull at Benares was when it ignored the ceremonies surrounding the eclipse of the sun, and calmly licked up the rice. Unlike men, animals do not drive themselves insane by the notions which they themselves invent; and down below the 'verminous realm of Original Sin' there is an underlying natural virtue which man can reach only by letting go his conscious mind and allowing the universe to think in his place.[16]

It is perhaps inevitable that this incipient pantheism, like the metaphysical optimism which it implies, should be neglected in the cinema, just as it was neglected in the very successful play which John Whiting wrote as an adaptation of *The Devils of Loudun* in 1961. What predominates on both stage and screen – and Huxley, it should be noted, greatly appreciated John Whiting's adaptation, which he saw on one of his rare visits to London[17] – is the physical horror of the events. What one remembers are the tortures, the hangings, the whippings, the hysteria, the giving of real enemas and the receiving of probably false stigmata, the heady mixture of sex and religion which continued to predominate after Huxley moved away from the novel and chose a *genre* which allowed a more natural blend between essays and narration. By concentrating on those aspects of seventeenth-century France which most anticipated the horrors of the twentieth century, he was also following the same bent of his own imagination which had led him to base the plot of *Point Counter Point* on a brutal murder and the death of a child, and which had struck D. H. Lawrence as so out of keeping with his professed humanism. In *The Devils of Loudun*, even the mystic, Father Surin, goes mad; and Huxley seems to have experienced, in the late forties and early fifties, so intense an onset of pessimism that his mystical beliefs became almost irrelevant to the world in which he and his contemporaries were forced to live.

9 Drugs, devils and biography

It is in the context of this increased pessimism that Huxley's famous first experiment with mescalin, on a 'bright November morning in 1953' is most immediately relevant to his career as a writer. He remarks almost casually in the opening pages of *The Doors of Perception* (1954) that he had never himself had a mystical experience, and his initial acceptance of 'the perennial philosophy' may well have been based much more on what he thought than on what he felt. It was, he wrote to a correspondent in 1945, through 'the aesthetic'[1] that he had come to the spiritual, and if he was only intellectually convinced of the views defended in the books he published after 1936, he would naturally have had difficulty translating them into the 'felt' medium of the novel. By the time he took mescalin Huxley was fifty-nine, and rather too set in his ways as a writer for the overwhelming experience which he describes in *The Doors of Perception* to have much effect upon the world vision expressed in his more imaginative works. Indeed, the similarities between *The Genius and the Goddess*, published only one year after *The Doors of Perception*, and novels such as *Point Counter Point* or *Time Must Have a Stop*, are so great that one wonders at times just how deeply Huxley the writer was affected by the drugs which he did so much to popularize.

Thus the narrator in *The Genius and the Goddess*, John Rivers, has the same kind of possessive, idealistic mother from whom Mark Rampion had succeeded in escaping in *Point Counter Point*, but who had rendered Brian Foxe so unfit for normal sexual emotions in *Eyeless in Gaza*. *The Genius and the Goddess* – like the early short story *Chawdron* 1936) – is told in flashback, and at the time when the events he describes take place, Rivers is working as research assistant to Henry Maartens, whose brilliance as a scientist and philosopher, contrasted with his inability to be anything but 'an idiot where human relations are concerned, a prize ass in all the practical affairs of life' again strikes a very familiar note. The central incident in *The Genius and the Goddess* again recalls some of Huxley's earlier insistence that what puritans call sexual immorality can well have much better results than rigid adherence to fixed rules. Henry Maartens is so parasitic upon his wife Katy that when she temporarily lacks the vigour to cure him by the sheer radiance of her presence, there seems to be no hope of saving him – until, that is, she comes to John Rivers's bedroom late one night. By going to bed with him, she renews contact with that 'animal grace' which represents the essential goodness of the purely physical universe, and adulterously uses her lover's vigour to cure her husband. Not only is this insistence on the beneficient power of amoral nature a very familiar theme in Huxley's work, dating back at least to his friendship with D. H. Lawrence in the nineteen-twenties. The very character of Katy Maartens is, as he later explained, based on that of Frieda Lawrence, and her relationship with Henry very similar to the one which Frieda had with Lawrence. On one occasion, as Huxley also points out in one of his letters, Frieda even 'raised Lawrence almost from the dead' when he was ill with influenza, and *The Genius and the Goddess* has more than a touch of the enthusiastic disciple who argued the case for 'the regulating body' in *Point Counter Point*. Yet the ending of the novel, in which the car that Katy is driving collides with a heavy lorry and her perfect body is 'destroyed with every refinement of physical outrage' is a reminder both of Huxley's obsession with blood and violence and of the constant defeat, throughout his fiction, of the spirit by the flesh.[2]

The Genius and the Goddess cannot, however, be dismissed simply because it presents basically the same world as *Crome Yellow* or *Point Counter Point*. What Laurence Brander calls Huxley's 'late flowering in his early sixties'[3] produced books whose virtues stand out most clearly if they are not set beside Huxley's other works, and this is particularly true of the analysis of sex and sexuality in *The Genius and the Goddess*. Yet while this analysis brings out both Huxley's tolerance and his liking for unusual psychological facts, it cannot fail to seem repetitive and almost obsessional when placed in the context of his other work. Thus in the safe next to his bed, Henry Maartens keeps 'all six copies of *The Psychology of Sex*, a copy of *Félicia* by Andréa de Nerciat and, published in Brussels, an anonymous work with illustrations entitled *Miss Floggy's Finishing School*'; and while it may be true, as John Rivers acknowledges as he looks back on what he was like when he first met Katy, that only 'a virgin prig of twenty-eight'[4] would be shocked by such a discovery, few readers of Huxley's other novels would share his surprise. Unorthodox sexual behaviour, especially with sado-masochistic overtones, recurs so frequently in Huxley's fictional universe, and if anything more insistently as he gets older, that its introduction into this story is less of a general psychological revelation than a reminder of how ambivalent Huxley's own attitude was towards the human body in general and physical sex in particular. His interest in algolagnia can indeed, as has already been suggested, be linked to that horror of physical suffering which lies at the heart of his agnosticism; and can, in turn, be traced back to the tragedies of his adolescence and early manhood. It can also, as it does in *After Many a Summer*, assume considerable philosophical significance when man's immense capacity for pain is both seen as biologically useless and contrasted with his more limited aptitude for pleasure. But when sado-masochism becomes, as it does here and elsewhere, a *tic* which makes Huxley almost as recognizable for his sexual preoccupations as Swift was for his obsession with excrement, the overall aesthetic quality of his work begins to suffer.

In *This Timeless Moment*, the memoir which Huxley's second wife, Laura Archera, published in 1969, there is a passage from an uncompleted novel on which he worked in the late nineteen-fifties. He was, as he remarked in a letter to Humphrey Osmond in 1955, interested in trying to find out why so many 'large areas of early life' were completely lost to him, and took two 400 mg capsules of LSD in an attempt to rediscover this lost childhood. All he experienced under the influence of the drug, however, was 'the direct, total awareness, from the inside, so to say, of Love as the primary and fundamental cosmic fact',[5] and he may well have begun the semi-autobiographical novel described in *This Timeless Moment* to see whether fiction could yield the recall which drugs denied. The proposed central character of this uncompleted novel, Edward Darnley, is certainly the kind of child who might grow up into a Philip Quarles or an Anthony Beavis. His intellectual precocity is sharply contrasted with his backwardness in 'self-control and the art of behaving like an English gentleman', and the main incident in the extracts published in Laura Archera's book describes an incident in his upbringing to which Huxley was clearly intending to attribute great importance. Edward has an 'enigmatic' German governess called Fräulein Lili who delights in smacking his bottom, and the similarity between this incident and Hugh Ledwidge's erotic rêveries about 'enemas and spankings' in *Eyeless in Gaza* could be interpreted in one of two ways. On the one hand, it could be argued that Huxley is merely following the well-established Freudian tradition whereby the adult but deviant sexual tastes of characters in novels are traced back to a childhood fixation described in the opening chapters. But, on the other hand, the general hostility which Huxley felt towards Freud is inconsistent with such an indiscriminate use of Freudian ideas; and the other similarities between Huxley himself and Hugh Ledwidge suggest that the frequency with which sado-masochism recurs in his fiction might perhaps originate from some curious experience in his own childhood.

Both in the final catastrophe of its plot and in its ambiguous attitude towards sex, *The Genius and the Goddess* is thus not funda-mentally different from the works which immediately preceded it. Even though her son Tommy escapes uninjured from the accident which kills both Katy Maartens and her daughter Ruth, he is merely being 'reserved for a worse death in Okinawa', and the potentially beneficent forces of nature have absolutely no long-term effects on general human experience. *The Devils of Loudun*, the book written immediately before the mescalin experiments, anticipates this very gloomy view of contemporary politics, with both sides in the cold war equally dominated by their self-made demoniacs, and in this respect *The Genius and the Goddess* shows little change from *Ape and Essence*, a 'vision of the future' which Huxley published in 1948, and whose prophecies make Orwell's *Nineteen eighty-four* seem like a picnic. Unlike most of his other books, however, *Ape and Essence* does throw some light on the kind of life which Huxley led in the nineteen-forties, and its initial setting in the Lou Lublin Productions film studios clearly owes a good deal to his work for the cinema both during and immediately after the second world war. As early as the nineteen-twenties, Huxley had shown a great interest in the cinema, and *Jesting Pilate* (1926) gives a fascinating glimpse of how, with Charlie Chaplin and Robert Nichols, he formed a Trinity of 'three grave theologians of art, too deeply absorbed in discovering the way of cinematographic salvation' to pay much attention to the Mack Sennett Bathing Beauties disposed around them on the beaches of the Pacific. After he had settled permanently in California in 1937, Huxley was inevitably drawn into the motion picture industry, and wrote at least three film scripts: a life of Madame Curie, which was not finally used, but for which he nevertheless received 15,000 dollars; an adaptation of *Pride and Prejudice*, which his colleagues at Metro Goldwyn Mayer always referred to as *Pee and Pee*, and which appeared in 1944; and a further adaptation, this time of *Jane Eyre*, in 1944.[6] The opening section of *Ape and Essence*, with its description of a lorry load of film scripts being taken off to the incinerator, may well be based upon experience, and certainly reflects some of the impatience which Huxley felt at the way his own work was hacked about in film studios. For in spite of his genuine interest in the cinema, he made it clear in a letter to Mrs Flora Strausse in 1941 that he accepted contracts for film scripts mainly because such work was 'on the whole preferable to the continual shallow improvising of articles and stories', and because he needed the money. Although his books sold consistently well, and *The Art of Seeing* enjoyed quite a remarkable success in 1943, Huxley was badly hit by wartime restrictions on printing and book production, and seems to have had few reserves to fall back on.

It would nevertheless be wrong to link the pessimism either of *Ape and Essence* – or, indeed, of any other book by Huxley – to his personal or financial problems. When, in 1950, his son Matthew married Ellen Hove, Huxley wrote to him that, 'after thirty years of it', he was 'definitely for matrimony', and the early difficulties of his married life, the 'dust crust' which characterized Philip Quarles's relationship with Elinor in *Point Counter Point*, had long since given way to a complete sympathy and understanding. Extraordinary though he found some of its inhabitants, Huxley enjoyed living in

California, especially in the nineteen-forties, when he and Maria had a house on the edge of the desert, and he was by no means in exile from the mainstream of European thought. His letters abound in references to the books he read, the interesting people he met, the scientific experiments which attracted his never-failing curiosity, and in spite of repeated illnesses – in 1943 he had a severe skin allergy, in 1949 a 'very tiresome' attack of bronchitis, in 1950 a touch of 'flu which led to 'a persistent discharge from the right sinus'[7] – the life he led was a full and happy one. What made the books he wrote in the nineteen-forties and nineteen-fifties so acutely pessimistic was something more impersonal: the impact of world events, and especially the multiplication, through science, of man's capacity for adding to the physical suffering already inseparable from all forms of life. The main action of *The Genius and the Goddess* takes place in 1921 – 'the days', as John Rivers puts it, 'when you could be a physicist without feeling guilty'.[8] In *Ape and Essence*, the researches in which Henry Maartens showed his genius have borne full fruit.

This novel-in-the-form-of-a-film-script is indeed a vision of the future which, like so much of Huxley's other work, makes the more insidious horrors of *Brave New World* seem positively attractive in comparison. The nuclear bombs dropped in 'those three bright summer days' of the third world war have not only destroyed most of the human race and driven the survivors back to barbarism. They have so poisoned life itself that children are born hopelessly deformed and the crops do not grow. Los Angeles, a city of two and a half million skeletons, supports a population of no more than a few thousand. Its libraries supply fuel for baking bread, while its inhabitants divide their time between finding clothes by digging up the well-preserved corpses in the many equivalents of Jo Stoyte's Beverley Pantheon and worshipping the Evil One, the Lord of the Flies, the Belial whose Guiding Hand has brought about these catastrophes and whose Providential Purpose is so obviously fulfilled by the effect of gamma rays on human genes. For, as the Arch-Vicar of this new religion so eloquently maintains, a man of science 'is bound to accept the working hypothesis that explains the facts most plausibly'. And what hypothesis other than diabolic intervention could explain the political disasters of the twentieth century? In AD 2108 – Huxley gives civilization 160 years to reach this state; the society of Brave New World took 720 years to attain its stability – Spandrell's hypothesis has indeed been verified, and in a form more terrible than even he could have imagined. 'In earth as it is in Hell', intones the Arch-Vicar; and his explanation, especially within Huxley's vision of the future, seems far more convincingly 'based on the facts of direct sense experience' than the mysticism of *The Perennial Philosophy*.

By AD 2108, however, the radio-active dust clouds have receded

H

enough to enable the inhabitants of New Zealand, spared the horrors of the third world war solely because their country had no strategic importance, to think of exploring what is left of North America. Prominent among the explorers is the botanist Dr Alfred ('stagnant') Poole, who gets separated from the main party and thus comes to play the same role of outsider as the Savage in *Brave New World*. He does, of course, know what has happened in history. Modestly, like Jeremy Pordage admitting to Mr Propter that he knows the mystics, 'would have thought himself most uncultured if he hadn't', he confesses to having read 'most of the obvious books on the subject': 'Graves's *Rise and Extinction of Russia*, for example; Basedow's *Collapse of Western Civilisation*; Bright's inimitable *Europe, An Autopsy*'; and Huxley's knack for mimicking the speech habits of intellectuals remains untouched by the gloom of his prophecies. What Dr Poole did not know, of course, before the Arch-Vicar explained it to him, was why it all happened, and his 'Liberal, Protestant views about the Devil' undergo considerable change as he learns to face the facts. Yet Belial's guiding hand does not do its work alone. Huxley had already shown himself a thinker ahead of his time when he made Lord Tantamount, in *Point Counter Point*, talk about the 'natural, cosmic revolution' which would take place if man continued to squander the mineral resources which had taken so many thousands of years to accumulate. In *Ape and Essence* this preoccupation has moved to the centre of his work and it is nowadays difficult to remember how unusual it was, in 1948, to describe the relationship between man and his environment as the parasitic one of 'tapeworm and infested dog, of fungus and blighted potato'.[9]

Possibly because he wished to compensate for the pessimism of this general diagnosis, Huxley gave *Ape and Essence* the only optimistic ending in the whole of his fiction. Just as promiscuity was mandatory in the Brave New World of AF 732, so monogamous sex is outlawed by the rulers of AD 2018; but in their society, copulation is permitted for only one fortnight a year. For the rest of the time, large *NO'S* attached to breast, buttocks and crutches remind both sexes of Belial's prohibition and ensure that energy – as in Orwell's *Nineteen eighty-four* – shall not be wasted on sex if it can be used for hatred. Dr Poole, however, decides to risk the punishment of being buried alive which hangs over every deviant couple, and escapes northwards to join the illegal, monogamous community called the Hots. Together with the girl with whom he has fallen in love (and with whom he goes beyond the 'innumerable erotic day-dreams' so often inspired by the 'spankings, sadly and prayerfully administered' by his mother) he sets out to cross the Mojave desert; and it is there that he finds, at the foot of a very large Joshua tree, the grave of the William Tallis who, in 1947, wrote the film script of

Ape and Essence. With the help of the duodecimo Shelley which he had saved from the ovens, he places the lines engraved on Tallis's tombstone in their correct, optimistic context, and silently breaks the white shell of a hard-boiled egg over the grave. Even if the Lord of the Flies triumphs and the predictions of *Ape and Essence* come true, Tallis will not have been wholly defeated. The only part of the universe we can meaningfully improve, insists Huxley, is ourselves, and the narrow circle of those with whom we come personally into contact; and by thus encouraging the lovers to escape into a community which defies the norms of AD 2018, Tallis has achieved all that lies within one man's power. Committed literature will not influence governments. Only individuals can be saved, and only by writers who have retained their own independence and originality.

It is naturally tempting to compare *Ape and Essence* with *Brave New World*. Both lay heavy emphasis on sex – and in *Ape and Essence* the whipping is even more insistent than at the end of *Brave New World* – both defend monogamy and both present contracting out of society as the only possible solution. On several occasions in his life, Huxley was tempted to belong to organizations which seemed sympathetic to his aims, and his membership of the Peace Pledge Union in the nineteen-thirties, like his initial acceptance of D. H. Lawrence's suggestion that he should join his colony in Florida, in 1917, shows that he was perhaps not always so much one of nature's non-joiners as one might suspect. But although he helped to write the prospectus for Trabucco College, a community founded by Gerald Heard, and spent a considerable amount of time there, he never actually became a member. As he wrote to Kingsley Martin, in July 1939, 'Religion can have no politics except the creation of small-scale societies of chosen individuals outside and on the margin of the essentially unviable large-scale societies, whose nature dooms them to self-frustration and suicide',[10] and there is almost a logical contradiction in forming a society to influence people only to declare it invalid if too many want to join. In 1946, Huxley assigned the royalties of *Science, Liberty and Peace* to the Quaker inspired Fellowship of Reconciliation, but once again refrained from actually becoming a member of the Society of Friends. Similarly, in 1954, he was so impressed by the work and methods of Dr Godel, the slightly unorthodox head of the Suez Canal Company's hospital of Ismalia, that he strongly recommended his son Matthew to go and work for him; but he did not go himself. Part of the impact which Krishnamurti had on him when they met in Switzerland in 1961 seems to have stemmed from the Indian mystic's uncompromising refusal to 'allow the poor *homme moyen sensuel* any escapes or surrogates, any *gurus*, saviours, *führers*, churches', and there can be few thinkers who insisted more than Huxley on the need for the individual to work out his own salvation with diligence – and to do it alone. Even recourse to drugs was strictly limited, and confined to those who were morally as well as physically suitable. In 1955, Huxley took mescalin only six times, and Laura Archera Huxley pointed out that the total amount of chemical absorbed by her husband between 1953 and 1963 was 'not so much as some people take to-day in a single week, sometimes in a single dose'.[11] Whatever influence his enthusiasm for LSD may subsequently have had upon the drug culture of southern California and elsewhere, Huxley himself remained as sensible and decorous in his personal behaviour as he had been in the days when he praised the English public-school system for its ability to provide the education suitable for an agnostic 'life-worshipper'.

This survival of Huxley's protestant conscience is evident even in the text of *The Doors of Perception*, where the one important reservation that he feels over the value of the experience concerns the fact that 'this participation in the manifest glory of things left no room, so to speak, for the ordinary, the necessary concerns of human existence, above all for concerns involving persons'. It is almost as if the revelations afforded by the drug had made Huxley conscious of the great objection to be levelled at the theory of mysticism set out in *Eyeless in Gaza* and *Grey Eminence*, and his very last novel, *Island*, certainly does try to present a more humane philosophy than any of Huxley's other mystical works. In the companion essay to *The Doors of Perception*, *Heaven and Hell*, Huxley also insists that mystical experiences can be expected to flow into the mind of someone taking the drug only if this person is 'philosophically and ethically prepared' for them, and there can be no question of mescalin providing a short cut into contemplative bliss. In this, as in other respects, it differs completely from the soma of *Brave New World*, which reduces rather than heightens consciousness, is biologically dangerous because it eventually shortens life, and whose 'three different effects – euphoric, hallucinant and sedative – were, as Huxley observed in 1963, 'an impossible combination'.[12] There are, of course, some common elements: soma and mescalin both free the mind from anxiety and neither of them – according to Huxley – causes a hang-over. Yet while soma gives rise only to a series of pleasant hallucinations, both mescalin and LSD – the claim is Huxley's, this time in a letter to Dr Humphrey Osmond, in 1955 – provide 'a realization why, in spite of everything, the universe is all right'. It had been under Dr Osmond's supervision – and in spite of the latter's sneaking fear that he might go down to history 'as the man who drove Aldous Huxley mad' – that Huxley had first taken mescalin, and it was in the letters between the two men that the word 'psychedelic' was first coined to describe the new mind-changing drugs. Huxley was certainly enthusiastic about their potentialities. In addition to their ability to release man from abstract ratiocination – and thus to enable him at one and the same time to 'survive as an animal' and yet 'think and feel as a human being' – mescalin and LSD both had great ecological and social advantages. Neither took up anything like the amount of good soil needed to produce alcohol or tobacco; and both produced results far superior to 'that state of uninhibited and belligerent euphoria which follows the ingestion of the third cocktail'.[13]

If one studies his remarks about it in more detail, however, mescalin reveals drawbacks, and its relative lack of effect on Huxley's fiction falls into place. 'Mescalin tends', he wrote in *Heaven and Hell*, in 1955, 'after ingestion to accumulate in the liver. If the liver is diseased, the associated mind may find itself in hell.' If this is so, then the mind is basically no freer from the body than it is either in the early short stories such as the Sir Hercules episode in *Crome Yellow* or in the more mature novels such as *Point Counter Point*. Man is still at the mercy of biological accident, just as he was when Thomas Henry Huxley reflected half humorously in his letter to Darwin that one might be foredoomed to lunacy because 'one's *nth* ancestor lived between tide-marks'. In 1942, in his *Evolution. A Modern Synthesis*, Sir Julian Huxley insisted that any purpose which we might read into evolution was only apparent, and wrote that it was 'just as much a product of blind forces as is the falling of a stone to earth or the ebb and flow of tides'.[14]

There is nothing in *The Doors of Perception* which can counterbalance the view that man is a biological accident, and when Huxley writes that the ultimate reality revealed through the mescalin experience is 'at once beautiful and appalling, but always other than human, always totally incomprehensible', he is unwittingly presenting, for the agnostic reader at any rate, an even gloomier vision of the human lot. At least for his brother and grandfather, experience could be analysed by science, and the 'how' of events tentatively understood, even if the 'why' remained for ever inaccessible. For Aldous, on the other hand, the final reply is ultimately that of the absurd and incomprehensible tyrant who answers out of the whirlwind and 'convinceth Job of ignorance and imbecillity', and he actually quotes the *Book of Job* to make his point clear.[15] The similarity between Huxley's mysticism and the essentially inhuman theology of Pascal or Kierkegaard thus recurs in *The Doors of Perception* even more explicitly than in *Time Must Have a Stop*, and this time accompanied by a form of double-think reminiscent of the central intellectual weakness in *The Perennial Philosophy*. For just as Huxley tried, when defending the general theory of mysticism, to combine a rejection of 'fruitless metaphysical questions' with a vocabulary that introduced purposes and goals at every turn, so he maintains that the world revealed by mescalin is at one and the same time 'always totally incomprehensible' and yet revelatory of 'the living, primordial cosmic fact of Love'. If there is love, it must surely manifest itself, as it does in traditional Christian theology, in essentially human terms. But if one holds, as does the Huxley of *Island* seven years after the publication of *The Doors of Perception*, that 'only God can make a microcephalous idiot', then it might be more consistent simply to say of mystical experiences, as did the Huxley of *Do What You Will* in 1929, that they 'happen because they do happen, because that is what the human mind is like'.[16]

The years immediately following the publication of *The Doors of Perception* were difficult for Huxley from a personal point of view, and this may well account for his failure to produce any major work between 1954 and 1961. In January 1952, Maria Huxley had had an operation for cancer of the breast, and six months later the disease recurred. She died in February 1955, assisted in her last moments by her husband's voice reminding her of the mystical experiences she had once had in the desert which she loved so much, and urging her to 'forget the body, to leave it lying there like a bundle of old clothes', to 'go forward into the light', where she would find 'only this pure being, this love, this joy'. Huxley's own description of how he helped her to die, to go 'deeper and deeper into the light, even deeper and deeper' is a most moving and beautiful piece of prose, and once again an indication, this time on the most important of all levels, of how very much better he often was as a man than as a writer.[17] For just as the absolute dependability which he showed in his friendship with D. H. Lawrence contrasted with the cold, amoeba-like qualities which he attributed to Philip Quarles, so the goodness and generosity stemming from him in his mature years quite outweigh the less attractive features of his later work. His personal relationships show no sign of the inadequacies he diagnosed so ruthlessly in his fictional characters, and the help which he was able to give others remained totally untouched by the intellectual weaknesses in his philosophy. The peyote-eating Indian, he writes in *The Doors of Perception*, 'has had the wit to protect his rear by supplementing the fig-leaf of a theology with the breech-clout of transcendental experience',[18] and Huxley's enthusiasm for mescalin perhaps stemmed from a feeling that his own theology was not quite adequate. When he reminded his wife, on her death-bed, of the actual experiences which she had had, rather than the views which they both held, he was again giving precedence to what is felt rather than what is thought. And it is curious how frequently ideas are made to give way to feelings in the work of this most intellectual of writers.

Another reason for Huxley's relative silence in the later nineteen-fifties lay in the time and energy consumed by the stage version of *The Genius and the Goddess*. *The Gioconda Smile*, an adaptation of an early short story, had enjoyed considerable success in both

London and New York in 1948 and 1950, and Huxley felt that the relative simplicity of *The Genius and the Goddess* also had dramatic potentialities. But although he wrote to his son and daughter-in-law as early as January 1955 that he was working on a dramatized version of the novel 'with an eye to production and, let us fervently hope, some Real Dough', the play was not finally produced until November 1957. Originally, Huxley chose Rita Allen and Joseph Anthony as producer and director of the play, but had to argue with them so much simply to maintain even the basic story line that he decided to put the work in other hands. Even then, however, he does not seem to have been able to find anyone prepared to keep the play as he and his collaborator, Beth Wendel, had written it; and the version of the play finally performed in New Haven and Philadelphia, in November 1957, was so far from his original conception that he tried, through his lawyer, to have his name removed from the credit titles.[19] Huxley was equally unfortunate, in 1956, in his attempts to arrange for the production of a musical comedy version of *Brave New World*, and here again he appears to have been the injured party. During his early years as a journalist, he had worked as an advertising copy-writer with *Vogue*, and acquired an ability to produce felicitously worded slogans which had been put to excellent use in the original novel. 'Was and will make me ill/I can take a gramme and only am' is a brilliant summary of the escape from time offered by soma, while the slogan 'One cubic centimetre cures ten gloomy sentiments' could interrupt two episodes of a television soap opera with no questions asked. The extracts from the proposed musical comedy version which he sent to Matthew and Ellen Huxley in September 1956 showed an equal facility for popularizing his social comments in snappily singable form, and there is even some irony in the fact that the Huxley who began his literary career as a rather sentimental poet should have used verse most effectively in apparently frivolous contexts. There is even greater irony, in view of its potentialities for the cinema, in the fact that Huxley should have sold the film rights for *Brave New World* to RKO almost as soon as the book came out in 1932. This studio, as Huxley pointed out in response to a query by Georges Neveux in 1962, did nothing with the rights but retain ownership of them, and Huxley certainly does not seem to have been very lucky in the attempts which he made to make more money from his work.[20] In 1940 the Pinker literary agency went into liquidation, after handling Huxley's literary affairs since 1921. Rather typically, Huxley emerged the poorer by £548, and the relative modesty of the sum involved helps to explain why he was always so anxious to do work that would bring in an immediate return. But he lacked the taste or the talent for self-advertisement which might have helped him to turn his ill-luck to advantage, and in 1954 he rejected the suggestion that he might co-operate in a *Huxley par lui-même* volume in the French *Ecrivains de Toujours* series. He had, he wrote to Jean Queval, a 'certain distaste for autobiography', so much so that he would find it 'extremely distasteful' to collaborate in writing a book about himself.[21]

There are nevertheless some unexpected sidelights to be gleaned from other people's comments upon Huxley, and which do not always fit in either with the self-portrait offered by his books or with the remarks he makes about himself in his letters. Thus it is impossible to imagine either Philip Quarles or Anthony Beavis as anything but most fastidious in their personal habits. Yet when Aldous went to stay with his brother Julian and his wife in the summer of 1950, Maria Huxley wrote to warn her sister-in-law to 'keep an eye on A's dirtiness and send his things to be pressed or cleaned as he never knows and is so untidy'. Similarly one would imagine that a man as intelligent as Huxley would realize when a theory was not working out quite so well as it should, and abandon it. But he remained convinced to the end of his days that the Bates system for eye-training was the only possible solution to the problem of poor sight, and this in spite of the fact that neither he nor Maria Huxley could ever find a number in a telephone directory. Neither were his attempts to avoid personal publicity always consistent or successful, and on one occasion his behaviour is difficult to reconcile with his frequent protestations of penury. In the nineteen-thirties, he and Maria Huxley lived in a flat in the Albany and posed for a photograph which appeared on the front page of *Vogue*. Convenient though this address was, as Maria remarked, for people who did all their shopping at Fortnum and Mason's,[22] there was some discrepancy between the values implied by such a preference and the philosophy of non-attachment developed in *Ends and Means*; and this flaunting of what one can only assume was transient affluence lent weight to the accusation that Huxley's pacifism was aimed at safeguarding the possessing class. Huxley's second marriage, to the author and violinist Laura Archera, in March 1956, was also accompanied by a certain amount of publicity, though this time through no fault of his own. The decision to have the ceremony conducted at the Drive-In Wedding Chapel, Yuma, Arizona, was inspired by what Huxley calls, in a letter to Anita Loos, his 'naïve hope' of being able to 'conduct his private affairs in privacy', but the news leaked out. Reporters swarmed round in such numbers that it would probably have been better, as he wryly observed, if they had had 'a slap-up affair at St Patrick's with Cardinal Spellman officiating and Claire Luce as bridesmaid'.[23]

Laura Archera was thirty-six when she married Huxley, and he was her first husband. It was, she points out in *This Timeless Moment*, a sign of Huxley's spontaneous charm that he prefaced his proposal to her with the question 'Have you ever been tempted by

marriage?', and thus instinctively avoided any embarrassing suggestion that she might have been left on the shelf. It was a happy
marriage, and seems in retrospect to have issued in a period of
Huxley's life in which his earlier, rather devastating brilliance
mellowed into a gentler awareness of how limited all human knowledge inevitably was. Sam Goldwyn – or perhaps Dorothy Thompson
– is said to have greeted Huxley on one occasion with the words
'Well, hello. I hear you're almost a genius', but jokes like this became
less appropriate when Huxley began to make remarks such as: 'It is
a little embarrassing that after forty-five years of research and study,
the best advice I can give to people is to be a little nicer to each
other.'[24] It was nevertheless during this period that Huxley became
increasingly regarded as a kind of universal sage, the man who
combined an encyclopaedic knowledge of art and science with an
immense compassion for the sufferings of mankind, and a thinker
whose zeal for mysticism went hand in hand with an intense awareness of how men could best survive on the planet which they were
so rapidly polluting. It is indeed these two concerns which dominate
in *Island*, a book snatched quite literally from the flames which
destroyed his house in California in May 1961, and is Huxley's final
attempt both to deal with the problems which had always obsessed
him as a writer as well as to suggest, through an ideal, how other
people might behave.

10 The problems of Utopia

In 1959 Huxley finally embarked upon the career which he had tried to adopt almost forty years previously: that of a University lecturer. He was invited, by the Santa Barbara Campus of the University of California, to give a series of lectures on *The Human Situation*, and did so in the spring and summer of that year. He endeavoured to deal, as he remarks in a letter to his son Matthew, with 'the biological foundations – the state of the planet, population, heredity in relation to environment', before discussing what he called 'the great determiner of modern civilization: technique in every field of human activity, and its effect on the social and political order'. As might be expected, the lectures proved immensely popular, attracting audiences of two thousand or more, and Huxley subsequently accepted comparable invitations at the Menninger Foundation, Topeka, at the Massachusetts Institute of Technology, and at Berkeley.[1] He had long since overcome the nervousness about speaking in public which had made him hesitate, in the nineteen-thirties, before giving lectures on pacifism, and developed an excellent technique. Neither, if one can judge from some notes which he made for a proposed travel book on California, did he always dwell exclusively on the drawbacks of the industrial civilization which had created so many refuges where its values could be called into question. 'The enormous affluence of the Western World', he commented in 1961, noting how 'all history was in paperbacks, all great music recorded, all art reproduced', 'is cultural as well as economic',[2] and his own career as a writer provides an indirect comment on how recent this affluence is. In the nineteen-twenties, Oxford was too poor to offer him a job, and he lived so much abroad partly because it was so much cheaper than in England. In the early nineteen-sixties, a writer with an eighth of the talent and knowledge which Huxley displayed in one volume of his early essays would not even have had to whistle. North American Graduate Schools would have spouted offers of Full Professorships involving only four hours teaching a week, and Huxley could have had all the leisure he so much envied Flaubert.

Although there are passages in *Island*, written during this period and published in March 1962, which do sound at times rather like lecture notes, the book itself is not quite the 'blue-print for survival' which Huxley's interest in ecology might lead one to expect. In spite of the fact that the quotation from Aristotle which he puts on the title-page states that 'In framing an ideal, we may assume what we wish, but should avoid impossibilities', *Island* formulates an ideal which is possible only in the sense that it contains no inner contra-

dictions, and Huxley makes it clear that the Western world is too far
gone to profit from his model. The action of the novel takes place in
Pala, an island somewhere in South East Asia, which has had an
extraordinary run of good luck. To begin with, it had the good
fortune not to be colonized by the Portuguese. It consequently never
had a Catholic minority preaching 'blasphemous nonsense about
it's being God's will that people should breed themselves into subhuman misery', and was able to adopt a sensible population policy.
The dominant religion happened to be Buddhism, and this not only
encouraged people to avoid 'putting superfluous victims' on to the
'Wheel of Birth and Death'; it also regarded the techniques of *coitus
reservatus* – 'what the Oneida community called Male Continence'
– as so orthodox that it gave it the name of *maithuna*, the 'yoga of
love'. For those unable to adopt this method, the postman now
brings 'a thirty-night supply of contraceptives' at the beginning of
each month, and Palanese good luck clearly extends to an unusual
menstrual cycle as well.[3]

Since their island escaped the Dutch and English as well as the
Portuguese, the Palanese also avoided the horrors of forced coloniza-
tion and the teachings of 'the man who invented Christianity – St
Paul'; and their ability to 'behave as if they were praeternaturally
sane and good' is very much a product of this particular accident.
Moreover, a non-Christian society has no need to accept traditional
family life, and Huxley neatly summarizes the drawbacks of the
nuclear family in an ironic recipe which captures all the horror of
modern city life: 'Take one sexually inept wage-slave, one dissatisfied
female, two or (if preferred) three small television addicts; marinate
in a mixture of Freudism and dilute Christianity; then bottle up
tightly in a four-room flat and stew for fifteen years in their own
juice.' The destruction of the family, so appalling a feature of *Brave
New World*, here takes on quite different overtones, and the development of what Huxley calls the Mutual Adoption Club enables each
child to feel secure in the affection and presence of twenty or so
adults while never being possessed by any of them. Freud and
Sophocles consequently reach Pala only to be laughed at, and the
plot of the 'marionette show *Oedipus in Pala*' ends with a boy and
girl managing to 'talk Jocasta out of suicide and Oedipus out of
hanging himself' by telling them 'not to be silly'. In a Mutual
Adoption Club, nobody knows exactly which adults are their
biological mother and father anyway, and no child is ever taught
'that horrible stuff about God getting furious with people every time
they make a mistake'.[4]

Both the mental and physical health of the Palanese thus stem
directly from the good fortune which enabled their ancestors to
avoid the two characteristically European ideologies of Christianity
and Freudianism, and there are other happy accidents in their

history which also saved them from Ford, Marx and Lenin. The mildness of the Palanese climate encouraged them in their conscious decision not to industrialize their economy, and they consequently avoided both capitalism and the growth of an urban proletariat. 'Lenin used to say', explains the reader's principal guide to Pala, Dr Robert MacPhail, 'that electricity plus socialism equals communism. Our equations are rather different. Electricity minus heavy industry equals democracy and plenty', and since the electric light 'doesn't belong to anybody' the Palanese have also had the unusual good fortune of achieving Communism without the class struggle.[5] Applied science is restricted to the solution of agricultural problems, and it is the passages in *Island* dealing with the correct use of land resources which probably reflect most closely the actual recommendations Huxley put into the lectures he gave at American universities. On a slightly different plane, *Island* is also full of suggestions about human genetics, and here again Huxley's ideas are not so Utopian as to be totally inapplicable to our world as we know it. While the general level of intelligence in the Western world, as Huxley argued as early as 1926, is steadily going down, the Palanese use of Deep Freeze and Artificial Insemination enables them to improve the quality of the race by ensuring that the most highly gifted male individuals in the past can still hand on their genes. Neither the isolation of the Palanese from the rest of the world nor their deeply held pacifism has prevented them from developing a series of techniques whereby young men can work out their aggression by rock-climbing and other dangerous sports, and Huxley's implied solution for the problems of vandalism shows a curious reversion to the once despised enthusiasms of his father. Palanese education is based upon a 'conservation-morality' which teaches that 'we shall be permitted to live on this planet only for so long as we treat all nature with compassion and intelligence', and Huxley's accompanying statement that 'Elementary ecology leads straight to elementary Buddhism' is perhaps the most persuasive of arguments in favour of the synthesis which he pursued for so long between the wisdom of the East and the scientific knowledge of the West.[6]

This description of a society in which 'the Fall is an exploded doctrine' also has some curious biographical overtones, and to some extent these are based on facts. The happiest accident in Pala's history was the arrival, in the early nineteen-forties, of Dr Andrew MacPhail, who had 'signed up as surgeon and naturalist on HMS *Melampus*, bound for the South Seas with orders to chart, survey, collect specimens and protect Protestant missionaries and British interests'. The similarity with the date and aims of the voyage on which Thomas Henry Huxley embarked, in 1846, on HMS *Rattlesnake* is quite remarkable, and the nature of Dr MacPhail's reading – eighteenth-century sceptics such as Gibbon and La Mettrie – also reflects something of the same cast of mind which led Aldous's grandfather to write a book on the philosopher Hume. The parallel is not, however, in any way an exact one, and Huxley chose the name MacPhail in order to express his admiration for 'the head of the United Fruit Company's hospital' at Quirigua, whom he had met during his travels in Central America in 1933.[7] The Dr MacPhail of *Island* also comes from a ferociously Calvinist background which bears no resemblance to Thomas Henry's obscure but rather non-descript upbringing, and the ideas which he introduces into Pala do not always have much in common with the strictly orthodox scientific approach which made Aldous's grandfather so formidable a controversialist. Thus he begins his career on the island by putting its ruler into a hypnotic trance while he operates on him to remove a tumour from the maxillary antrum – Huxley here pays tribute to the work of the real James Esdaile under the pseudonym of Professor Elliotson – and then proceeds, with the help of his grateful patient, to take the island under his control. He enhances his prestige by using hypnotism to introduce painless childbirth as well as 'painless operations for stones, cataracts and haemorrhoids', introduces scientific farming, and combines the establishment of English as Pala's second major language with the continued exclusion of all European traders or explorers. And not only does Dr MacPhail begin the alliance between East and West which gives Palanese civilization its true quality.[8] He also leaves children to carry on the good work, and it is they who still constitute what one is tempted to call the *eminences grises* of the official Palanese government. For *Island* is not simply an impersonal statement of the kind of society which Huxley the mystic and conservationist would have liked to see created by the systematic avoidance of the general errors of the past. It is also a vision of what the Huxley family might have helped to achieve if Thomas Henry had thought in the nineteenth century as his grandson came to think in the twentieth. It is almost as if, by the invention of Andrew MacPhail, Huxley were paying a last tribute to the grandfather whom he so often resembled, while at the same time suggesting that the metaphysical problems which Thomas Henry bequeathed to his descendants might yet receive a solution.

In this respect, however, the pattern of events described in *Island* is less reassuring than the general ideas which the novel puts forward. MacPhail's Pala is no less vulnerable than the castle of Sir Hercules Lapith, in *Crome Yellow*, to the assaults of the outside world, and the extraordinary run of luck which has enabled a genuinely human civilization to develop is brought to a disastrous end. Once again, moreover, it is a brutish young man who wrecks the paradise. Murugan Mailenda, son of the present Queen Mother of Rana, is due to succeed to the throne on his eighteenth birthday, and he has no sympathy for any of Rana's achievements. His homosexuality, direct consequence of his mother's highly possessive love, not only makes him scorn the sexual delights of Palanese civilization. It also leads to an intense admiration for the aggressively virile ruler of the neighbouring island, Colonel Dipa, whose enthusiasm for tanks, guns and oil knows no bounds. Together, he and Murugan organize a 'liberating invasion' which at long last makes the oil in which Pala is so rich available for foreign companies; and the novel thus ends with another defeat of the spirit by the flesh. Moreover, by yet another reversion to the patterns of Huxley's earlier fiction, Murugan and Dipa are aided and abetted in their evil doings by the only genuinely European in the novel, the journalist and writer Will Farnaby. It is his accidental arrival on the island which supplies the pretext for the guided tour – he is, in this respect a cynical Savage, a disillusioned Dr Poole – and it is he who acts as middleman between Murugan and Jo Aldehyde, the financier who wants to get his hands on Pala's oil. His realization of the immense value of the civilization he helps to destroy comes too late, and in this again he marks a return to the heroes of an earlier period, the Anthony Beavis of *Eyeless in Gaza* or the Sebastian Barnack of *Time Must Have a Stop*. They too were men who 'saw the best and approved of it; but followed the worst', and Will Farnaby has the same Baudelairean inability as Sebastian Barnack to go to bed with the women he admires or to admire the women with whom he goes to bed. Intellectually, Huxley clearly disapproves of him, and the portrait of the 'man who would not take "Yes" for an answer' is his final verdict on the Jesting Pilate that he himself once was. But the world which Farnaby both symbolizes and detests enjoys a triumph at the end of *Island* which recalls the victory of Spandrell in *Point Counter Point* or Dr Obispo in *After Many a Summer*. Only the mynah birds, whose incessant cry of 'Karuna, Karuna', calls attention to the here and now, to the mystical experience available to man in this world, carry a reminder of what human beings can – with luck – achieve.

It is perhaps unfair to criticize Huxley's utopia because it is defeated. A writer has to end a book somehow, and it is much easier to do so, aesthetically speaking, by a catastrophe. Yet although Palanese civilization does not collapse through any internal weakness – except, perhaps, in showing too great a trust in visiting outsiders – the solution which it presents to the recurrent problems in Huxley's work is still not wholly satisfactory. Admittedly, the Palanese are not torn between the body and the spirit, and are not alienated either by their intellects or their sexual appetites. *Coitus reservatus* is not only a contraceptive technique. It also implies, for the man, an inhibition of the natural instincts to the point where the hope voiced in one of Huxley's earliest poems is realized, and the mind is no longer 'in bondage to brute things'.[9] Unlike Lucy Tantamount, Helen Amberley and Will Farnaby's mistress Babs, the women in Pala are not subject to the whims of 'a body agonising in the extremity of pleasure', and for the first time in Huxley's work, sex is presented as a wholly laudable activity. But John Humphrey Noyes, on whose example Huxley most relies for his praise of Male Continence, eventually fathered eight children after the age of fifty-eight, and for once it is possible to fault one of Huxley's nostrums with quite indubitable evidence.[10] And although he insists through-out the novel that the Palanese are free, he does not say what this freedom means for anyone who happens not to like the values on which Palanese society is based. Is such a person going to be allowed to try to change them? Would the one newspaper in Pala, run by 'a panel of editors representing half a dozen different parties or interest', agree to publish Huxley's pet hatred – Sears, Roebuck, and Co.'s *Spring and Summer Catalog*?[11] Unless it did, the much vaunted freedom of the Palanese would be little better than the more obviously conditioned reflexes of *Brave New World*. But if it did, would Palanese society stand the strain?

Yet these are minor quibbles, points that a Philip Quarles or an Anthony Beavis might make. The real question in *Island* is whether or not Huxley overcomes what he himself calls, in the text of the novel, the 'Essential Horror': the fact that both animals and human beings die of appalling diseases, that the mind is defeated by the body, that 'only God can make a microcephalous idiot'. For when, towards the end of the novel, Will Farnaby takes the '*moshka* medicine', the 'truth and beauty drug' which brings him into direct contact with God, with what Eckhart called 'Felicity so ravishing, so inconceivably intense that no one can describe it', he proceeds to discuss it in intellectual terms with Susila MacPhail, his chief guide to this aspect of Palanese life. God, she explains to him, had himself been enjoying such felicity for untold ages when 'all of a sudden, up comes Homo Sapiens, out comes the knowledge of good and evil', and the very nature of the ultimate experience changes. God has to 'switch to a much less palatable kind of fruit', the knowledge which he has of himself through the human beings in whom he is now immanent. The whole burden of her remarks is that human exis-tence, far from having been willed by God, is a rather unfortunate mistake, and Huxley's own comment, in *The Perennial Philosophy*, that 'to some extent, creation *is* the Fall' suggests that this is an idea which he accepts. Such a view is certainly consistent with the Buddhist readiness to accept birth control on the grounds that 'begetting is merely postponed assassination', and that everyone should do his best to 'get off the Wheel of birth and death'. Whether it diminishes the 'Essential Horror' is nevertheless another question.[12]

Laura Archera Huxley complained in 1969 that *Island* had been 'little publicized and grossly misunderstood', and it is certainly true that few readers and even fewer critics would give it the palm over

Brave New World. It is difficult for an English or American reader to be very enthusiastic over a book which presents him with a paradise only to exclude him from it on the grounds that his culture is 'too irretrievably committed to applied physics and chemistry with all their dismal consequences, military, social and political'.[13] It is also hard to reconcile the view of human existence as a mistake with the statement which, according to *This Timeless Moment*, Huxley frequently used as an opening for his lecture on human potentialities: 'As an act of faith, and I think it is an act of faith shared by most people who are concerned with human decency and liberty, I believe that man is here for the purpose of realizing as much as possible of his desirable potentialities within a stable and yet elastic society.' The vision of man as a biological sport is fully consistent with a rational attempt to improve human existence; and there is no logical contradiction between the exclusion of all idea of transcendental purpose and a determined effort to make the universe slightly less absurd. Similarly, although the evidence for such a belief is scanty, there is no reason why a social reformer should not derive encouragement from the notion that the world is governed by a wise and beneficent deity who created mankind in His own image. What is untenable, on purely logical grounds, is the view which proclaims that it would have been better if human beings had never existed and yet insists that they should act morally in order to fulfil God's purposes here on earth.

'Born in an age of faith', wrote Alexander Henderson in the first full-length study of his work, 'Huxley would have been the most famous of divines, famous for his learning and his eloquence', and his basically religious cast of mind is visible even in his humanist period. *Do What You Will* is a collection of what Thomas Henry Huxley would have called 'lay sermons', and only in *Crome Yellow* did Huxley completely resist the temptation to preach. But the sermons of a man born in an age of unbelief inevitably reflect the contradictions of that age, and the religion which Huxley finally professed has the paradoxical quality of so underlining the weaknesses of the apologist's case that intellectual belief becomes quite impossible. In this respect, it is undoubtedly by accident that he becomes a 'leader of modern thought', and the fact that he wrote fiction as well as essays again heightens the contradictory nature of his work. For whether he is writing as an agnostic humanist or a mystical believer, the patterns of Huxley's novels invariably contradict the hopes and findings of Huxley the essayist, and *Island* is no more an exception than *Point Counter Point*. But there was a stoic as well as a mystic in Huxley, and he never whined. Neither the explicit statement, in *Those Barren Leaves*, that the body always killed the spirit, nor the less conscious recognition, in *The Genius and the Goddess* or *Island*, that neither natural nor divine grace can ever win, was an appeal for personal sympathy. The romantic temperament was as absent from Huxley's work as it was from his life, and his behaviour in the last years as worthy of the stoic he had always been as of the mystic he had striven to become.

'People ask me', writes Max Cutler, the doctor who attended him in his final illness, 'how Aldous faced death. He faced it as he faced life: with dignity and courage.'[14] In May 1961, just as he was starting to write *Island*, Huxley learned that he had cancer of the tongue. He refused surgery, and the growth was temporarily arrested by radium needle treatment. The novel was almost completed when his house, at 3276 Deronda Drive, Los Angeles, caught fire on a night of high wind, and all his and Laura's belongings, except for a few clothes, the typescript of *Island*, her Guarneri violin, and their motor-car, were destroyed in the blaze. When *Time* magazine wrote that 'while firemen restrained the nearly blind British author from running into the blaze, Huxley wept like a child', the social satirist in him was temporarily reborn. The firemen, he pointed out in a letter to the magazine, arrived well after the television cameras, too late to do anything. Huxley the realist, who had earlier given his son some useful advice on the tax advantages of American endowment schemes over English ones, commented that 'the difference between the insurance payment and the real loss . . . can be taken off one's taxes'. While to Robert Hutchins, Huxley the stoic philosopher remarked that he was evidently 'intended to learn, a little before the final denudation, that you can't take it with you'.[15] However changed his intellectual attitude might have been, Huxley the sixty-year-old man reacted to personal disaster with the same blend of good humour and common sense as the sixteen-year-old schoolboy, and when cancer recurred in 1962 and 1963, there was no 'rage against the dying of the light'. He continued to write and work up to the very end, and the last part of his essay *Shakespeare and Religion* was dictated the day before he died. In 1960 he had described to Dr Humphrey Osmond how his own experience at Maria's death-bed had convinced him that 'the living can do a great deal to make the passage easier for the dying, to raise the most purely physiological act of human existence to the level of consciousness and even spirituality', and the circumstances of his own death reflected that belief. In *Island*, Dr Robert MacPhail's wife Lakshmi dies in her husband's arms, comforted by the same words that Huxley had whispered to Maria when she was dying. Some hours before his death, Huxley asked Laura Archera to give him an injection of 'LSD 100 mm intramuscular', and she herself comments on how 'once again, he was doing what he had written in *Island*'. 'He had taken the *moksha* medicine in which he believed', she writes, and this first use of LSD to ease the pain of dying gave the results for which both she and he had hoped.[16] He died in peace, at 5.20 on the afternoon of 22 November 1963.

I

Notes and references

Except where otherwise stated, references to Huxley's works are made to the Chatto and Windus *Collected Edition*, published from 1946 onwards. The following abbreviations are used: AA – *Adonis and the Alphabet*; AE – *Ape and Essence*; AH – *Antic Hay*; AMS – *After Many a Summer*; AR – *Along the Road*; BL – *Those Barren Leaves*; BMB – *Beyond the Mexique Bay*; BNW – *Brave New World*; CW – Chatto and Windus; CY – *Crome Yellow*; DL – *Devils of Loudun*; DP – *The Doors of Perception*; DWYW – *Do What You Will*; EG – *Eyeless in Gaza*; EM – *Ends and Means*; GE – *Grey Eminence*; GG – *The Genius and the Goddess*; HH – *Heaven and Hell*; JP – *Jesting Pilate*; MV – Memorial Volume, edited by Sir Julian Huxley, CW 1965; PCP – *Point Counter Point*; PP – *The Perennial Philosophy*; TMHS – *Time Must Have a Stop*.

Introduction

1 AH 9, EG (quoted throughout in the Penguin edition) 25.
2 BL (quoted throughout in the Penguin edition) 279.
3 Ronald Clark, *The Huxleys*, Heinemann, 1968, p. 143.
4 *The Letters of Aldous Huxley*, edited by Grover Smith, Chatto and Windus, 1969, p. 61.

Chapter 1

1 See Gervas Huxley, *Both Hands. An Autobiography*, Chatto and Windus, 1970, p. 17.
2 AA 37, CW 1956.
3 Ronald Clark, *The Huxleys*, Heinemann, 1968, p. 151.
4 DWYW 227 (quoted throughout in the Thinkers' Library edition, Watts and Co., 1936); BMB 92.
5 *The Letters of Aldous Huxley*, edited by Grover Smith, Chatto and Windus, 1969, p. 609.
6 *This Timeless Moment*, Laura Archera Huxley, *A Personal View of Aldous Huxley*, Chatto and Windus, 1969, p. 185; EG 42.
7 Gervas Huxley, *op. cit.*, p. 67.
8 AR 13.
9 JP 103. When he described himself (*Letters*, p. 589) as having been 'born near the end of one of history's rare Golden Ages', Huxley was contrasting the relative security of nineteenth-century middle-class civilization with the violence of the twentieth century.
10 *Letters*, 101. For Huxley's dislike of Queen's College, full, in October, 1915 of 'black men and Americans of the name of Schnitzenbaum and Fischmacher and Schnoppelganger-Fleischmann', see p. 84; rooms in Oxford – MV 60–1.
11 AH 20.
12 BL 92 (quoted throughout in the Penguin edition, 1951); AR 80 ('Was hard work to the glory of God more detestable than eight

hours a day in an office to the greater enrichment of the Jews') shows this side of Chellifer's character to be autobiographical as well.

13 See *The Life and Letters of Thomas Henry Huxley*, edited by his son (Macmillan, 1900), Vol. I, p. 162. Letter dated 1.1.59.

14 See *The London Magazine*, August 1955; and Michael Holroyd, *Lytton Strachey, A Critical Biography*, Heinemann, 1968, Vol. II, p. 363.

15 Clark, *op. cit.*, p. 211.

16 Gervas Huxley, *op. cit.*, p. 67; Clark, *op. cit.*, p. 30. According to his obituary in *The Times* (4.5.33), Leonard Huxley 'when a boy, rode over most of Europe on one of the old, high bicycles'.

17 BL 103–4.

18 EG 122–3 (quoted throughout in the Penguin edition, 1955).

19 Clark, *op. cit.*, pp. 140–1, 165, 211.

20 See *The Collected Letters of D. H. Lawrence*, edited by Harry T. Moore, Heinemann, 1962, pp. 1125, 1177.

21 Connolly, *The Condemned Playground*, Routledge, 1945, p. 115.

22 *The Criterion* (described by D. H. Lawrence in *op. cit.*, p. 1125, as 'that expensive and stewed T. S. Eliot Quarterly'), Vol. IX, p. 373. This hostility does not, however, seem to have been ideological, since Hamish Miles praised DWYW in Vol. IX, pp. 343–5, and wrote of the 'clarity and above all the rhetorical beauty' of its expression.

23 Vol. XLV, pp. 344–7.

24 *Letters*, p. 291 and *The Letters of D. H. Lawrence, op. cit.*, 1049.

25 *Letters*, p. 379. Similarly, in 1936, Huxley wrote to C. E. M. Joad, of EG, that 'wolves at doors imposed immediate publication and I let it go, feeling uncomfortably in the dark about the thing'.

Chapter 2

1 Eliot in MV p. 30; the poem was first published in *Leda and other poems*, in 1920; it was republished in *Selected poems*, in 1925; in the Everyman edition of Huxley's *Stories, Essays and Poems*, in 1937; in *Verses and Comedy*, in 1946; and in *The Collected Poetry of Aldous Huxley*, edited by Donald Watt, in 1971.

2 Quoted from *Laughter in the Next Room*. See John Atkins, *Aldous Huxley, a literary study*, John Calder, 1956, pp. 19–20; Roy Campbell – see Clark, *op. cit.*, p. 212.

3 PCP 301.

4 *The First Lady Chatterley*, The Dial Press, Sydney, 1944, p. 26.

5 CY 110; BL 258.

6 AH 183 and BL 242. For Huxley's own opposition to the Freudian view of art, see AR 165.

7 CY 56–9. Huxley himself points out that this is based upon an actual pamphlet called *The Significance of Air War*, by the Rev. E. H. Horne, published in 1916; see also GE 223 'God the avenger might have his reasons for wishing to destroy a large number of central Europeans.'

8 BL 159.

9 GE 223; see also PCP 319; EG 95, 143, 177; PP 116; AMS 202.

10 *Life and Letters*, Vol. I, p. 220.

11 *ibid.*, Vol. I, p. 359, letter dated 20.2.71; Tennyson, *In Memoriam*, stanza LV; the *Fifth Philosopher's Song* was written as early as July 1918, when Huxley sent it to Julian with the comment about Tennyson (*Letters*, p. 158).

12 BL 268–9.

13 *Dilemmas*, Cambridge University Press, 1954. Paperback, pp. 68–81, 76.

14 *Island* (quoted throughout in the Penguin edition, 1964), 243.

15 *The Claxtons.* See Everyman edition of the *Stories, Essays and Poems*, Dent, 1937. The story first appeared in *Brief Candles*, 1930.

16 *Young Archimedes* was published in *Little Mexican*, in 1924. For autobiographical background, see *Letters* 217–18. According to Clark, *op. cit.*, p. 217, *The Farcical History of Richard Greenow* has 'almost painful overtones of thinly disguised family history'.

17 PCP 410, 561; see also BL 84, and TMHS 305 'Being identical with their physiology, they *know* there's a cosmic order.' (TMHS is quoted the 1966 edition of *The Collected Works of Aldous Huxley*.)

18 BL 79.

19 BL 279; BL 255.

20 AH 254.

21 AH 168–9, 134–5.

22 BL 310, 312.

Chapter 3

1 Clark, *op. cit.*, p. 227. Huxley was not an uncritical reader of the *Encyclopedia Britannica*, and in BMB 114 anticipated the tone of the more detailed criticisms put forward by Harvey Einbinder in *Encounter* for May 1961. AR 71. There is also a striking resemblance between Huxley's remarks about a 'learned madman' and Sartre's creation, in 1938, of l'Autodicate in *La Nausée*, a lawyer's clerk educating himself by reading all the books in the public library in alphabetical order.

2 Clark, *op. cit.*, *idem.* Also reflected in PCP 448, where little Phil stays at home while his parents go on a round the world cruise.

3 JP 214, 120; see also TS 305 and AMS 212, where 'harmless animality' enables four-fifths of the population to get through life without going to a lunatic asylum.

4 JP 42, 160, 127.

5 See Huxley's preface to his edition of Lawrence's *Letters* (1932), reprinted from *The Olive Tree* (1936) in the Everyman *Stories, Essays and Poems*, 1937, p. 336.

6 Clark, *op. cit.*, pp. 223–4; Richard Mayne, *Encounter*, February 1972; according to Naomi Mitchison (MV 53), another model for Lord Edward was her father. A possible model for a female character in Huxley's fiction is his mother-in-law, of whom he wrote in 1960 that she 'flourished under the stimulation of successive disasters in France – the death of Camus, and now, very belatedly, the Fréjus dam break' (*Letters*, 885). This may have been a long-standing characteristic which suggested the person of the Queen Mother in TMHS, who outlives everyone and seems to rejoice in disaster (pp. 150–1).

7 PCP 291. For Lawrence's comment on Rampion see his letter to Huxley, dated 28.10.28, *op. cit.*, p. 1096.

8 PCP 444.

9 Laura Archera Huxley, *op. cit.*, p. 274; J. S. Fraser, *The Modern Writer and his World*, Verschoyle, 1953, p. 93.

10 PCP 224 (no maid); 433 (dancing with professional); on 7.2.29 Lawrence wrote to E. H. and A. Brewster that 'the love affair with Lucy was —'s affair with —', *op. cit.*, p. 1125.

11 PCP 408 (musicalization); 576 (very possession of a soul).

12 *Letters* 373.

13 Letter dated 28.10.28, *op. cit.*, p. 1096; Huxley's comment on 'grinning blackamoors' is in AH 168–9; on 'repulsive German Jews' in *Letters* 171.

14 Strachey – quoted by Alexander Henderson, *Aldous Huxley*, Russell and Russell, U.S.A., 1964, p. 5. Mr Henderson's study was originally published by Chatto and Windus, in 1936, and was the first book to appear on Huxley's work. John McCormick, *Catastrophe and Imagination*, Longmans, 1957, p. 286.

15 PCP 433–4; see *Pensées*, Lafuma, 136.

16 PCP 497; see *Fusées*, Pléiade edition of Baudelaire's *Oeuvres complètes*, 1963, p. 1249.

17 See Lawrence's letter of 1.2.29 to S. S. Koteliansky, *op. cit.*, p. 1122. Mosley was Chancellor of the Duchy of Lancaster in 1929. He founded the 'New Party' in 1930; and the British Union of Fascists (foreshadowed in PCP by the British Freemen) in 1932.

18 PCP 213, when Philip Quarles comments: 'How furious he gets with old Mach! They're undermining his simple faith. They're telling him that the laws of nature are useful conventions of strictly human manufacture and that space and time and mass themselves, the whole universe of Newton and his successors, are simply our own invention.'

19 Interview in *Le Monde*, 18.4.64.

20 PCP 2 and 205.

21 CY I; PCP 537.

22 *Limbo* 172.

23 DWYW 209.

24 *Themes and Variations*, CW 1950, p. 2.

25 *Letters*, 656; for Rampion's view, PCP 561.

26 *Letters*, 740 and 868. For another similarity see T. H. Huxley's remark 'As a child, my love for her [=his mother] was a passion,' *Life and Letters*, Vol. I, p. 4.

27 Quoted by Mrs Q. D. Leavis in *Scrutiny*, Vol. V, no. 2, September 1936, pp. 179–81.

28 *Scrutiny*, Vol. I, pp. 273–9.

29 Quoted by John Atkins, *op. cit.*, p. 216.

Chapter 4

1 Quoted by Ronald Clark, *op. cit.*, p. 74. Mr Clark has very generously supplemented his remark by the information that the letter was written on 18 August 1858 – that is to say before T. H. Huxley's family grew to seven children between 1858 and 1865.

2 AR 63; AA 77; Lord Tantamount (according to Ronald Clark, *op. cit.*, based upon John Scott Haldane, J. B. S. Haldane's father). PCP 25, 80; comment on Gandhi DWYW 68.

3 *Island*, p. 84. See also p. 59 in same book: 'By 1930, any clear-sighted observer could have seen that for three quarters of the human race, freedom and happiness were almost out of the question'; see also the chapter on population in *Brave New World Revisited*, CW 1964, pp. 11–23.

4 CY 28, 130; BL 91; in *Brave New World Revisited*, Huxley writes (p. 11): 'I forget the exact date of the events recorded in *Brave New World*; but it was somewhere in the sixth or seventh century A.F. (After Ford).'

5 Bertrand Russell, *The Scientific Outlook*, Allen and Unwin, 1931, p. 221. I am indebted to Peter Bowering's study of Huxley's novels for having drawn my attention to this parallel.

6 MV 22.

7 Krishnamurti – quoted by Atkins, *op. cit.*, p. 183; BNW 16.

8 *Nature*, 23 April 1932, pp. 597–8.

9 Joseph Needham – *Scrutiny*, Vol. I, no. 1, May 1933, pp. 76–9.

10 Published as the closing essay in a collection edited by Julian Huxley under the title *The Humanist Frame*, Allen and Unwin, 1961. Farcical History – see *Limbo*, pp. 66–8.

11 *The Times*, 25.11.63. Other critics to notice the Victorian side of Huxley's personality include the reviewer in the *TLS* for 12.8.55. who wrote in his account of GG that Huxley had remained 'curiously Victorian'; Frank Swinnerton, who notes a letter describing Huxley's 'Victorian giggle' (*Figures in the Foreground*, Hutchinson, 1963, p. 188); Laurence Brander, *op. cit.*, p. 191, who attributes the fact that Huxley was 'disappointed' in LSD to the 'recurring concern about social responsibility' stemming from his 'inability to get away from himself and his Victorian forebears'; and Clark, *op. cit.*, p. 220, who calls him 'the last of the Victorians'.

12 See *The Times*, 18.1.33. The ban was lifted on 29.3.37. In 1947, one of my uncles reproved me for reading PCP and recommended Jeffrey Farnol as a healthier alternative.

13 PP 25. The remark is most appropriate to the financial support given to Arts Faculties in British Universities.

14 Foreword to the 1946 edition of BNW. See Penguin Classics, 1955, p. 8.

Chapter 5

1 DWYW 172; novels of disillusion – see Graves and Hodge, *The Long Week-end*, Faber and Faber, 1941, p. 147.

2 BMB 74, 92, 112. *Sermons in Cats* first appeared in *Music at Night* in 1931. See p. 260 of the CW 1960 edition where Huxley attributes the original advice to Ronald Firbank who 'once told me that he wanted to write a novel about life in Mayfair and so was first off to the West Indies to look for copy among the negroes'. For Firbank's influence on Huxley's early novels, see I. S. Fraser, *op. cit.*, p. 93; and Cyril Connolly, *op. cit.*, p. 114, 'during the twenties, it was almost impossible for the average clever young man not to imitate him (i.e. Huxley) – just as he had once imitated Norman Douglas, Firbank and Eliot.

3 *What Are You Going To Do About It?* is most conveniently studied in the Everyman edition of Huxley's *Stories, Essays and Poems*, Dent, 1937, republished 1954, pp. 380–406. It was originally published by Chatto and Windus, under the auspices of the Peace Pledge Union in 1936 under the title *The Case for Constructive Peace*, at 3d. Cecil Day Lewis's pamphlet *We're Not Going To Do NOTHING* was published by The Left Review and cost 6d.

4 *The Times*, 30.4.36 and 19.9.36.

5 See *Letters*, 169–70; 451; 479–80; 483; 503–5; 511; 531. Conquered wheatlands, 528.

6 *The Times*, 19.6.36.

7 EM (quoted in the CW 1937 edition) 273.

8 Sir Julian Huxley's *Memories* was published by Allen and Unwin in 1970. The account of Trevenen's death is on pp. 101–2.

9 BL 30–1. For Huxley's remarks about his aunt, see *Writers at Work*, The Paris Interviews, Secker and Warburg, 1963, pp. 161–86.

10 *Letters*, 408–9.

11 EG 255; see *The Times*, 4.5.33.

12 *Letters*, 224. Huxley's own comments on *Antic Hay* provide a better guide to its value than any critic has so far offered. It was, he wrote to his father on 26.11.23 (*Letters*, 224), 'a very serious book' which had 'artistically [. . .] a certain novelty, being a work in which all the ordinarily separated categories – tragic, comic, fantastic, realistic – are combined so to speak chemically into a single entity'.

13 DWYW 179. According to Edmund Wilson's *The Shores of Light*, Strauss and Young, 1952, p. 567, *Les Conquérants* was originally translated at Huxley's instigation, but did not receive a great deal of recognition from the English-speaking public.

14 For Miller's remarks, see EG 343–4. According to Laura Archera Huxley, Aldous became a vegetarian in the nineteen-thirties because it suited his digestion (*op. cit.*, p. 110). For his unorthodox remedies and beliefs, see *Letters*, 402, 482, 499, 696, 864.

15 See *Life and Letters of T. H. Huxley*, Vol. I, p. 8. For Huxley's comments on Bates, see *Letters*, 468; views on fashions in medicine, 489.

16 *Letters*, 444; GE 98.

17 *Scrutiny*, Vol. V, no. 2, pp. 179–81. For Miller on men and insects, see EG 342, and Huxley's 'novel about problem of freedom', *Letters*, 385; for the Baudelairean 'torture of pleasure' see EG 16, 291, 305; and for comparable expressions elsewhere, AH 240, BL 226 and 292, PCP 497 (of Lucy Tantamount), *Island*, 81 and 240.

18 *The Times*, 19.6.36.

19 *op. cit.*, p. 226; for Mr Propter's views see AMS 182.

20 See Robert Craft's article in *Encounter*, November 1965, pp. 101–16; for the picnic, see Anita Loos's essay in MV, pp. 91–3.

21 MV 141.

Chapter 6

1 DWYW 37.

2 DWYW 15, 12; EM 283.

3 EM 286, 298.

4 DWYW 43. *Letters*, 576. See also *Letters*, 646 for the comparable view, expressed in 1952, that 'many of the world's artistic and cultural organisations are infiltrated by homosexuals, with the result that nobody who is vulgar enough to like women stands a chance'.

5 JP 214, EM 282, DWYW 97, EM 300, 196, DWYW.

6 *Letters*, 779, 938 and AA 71; Spandrell, PCP 307.

7 PP 345 (free mind); 337 (society); 72; 209 and 273 (cosmic intelligence test); 72 (infinite number of points); 31 (divine serenity); 69 (Ruysbroeck); Huxley comments in *Letters*, 532 and 534.

8 *TLS*, 2.11.46.

9 'Footless question' PP 232; Rhine – *Letters*, 484.

10 PP 232, 272.

11 PP 97 (deep-seated will); 55 (final end). The question which begins the 'shorter catechism' is 'What is the chief end of man' and the reply 'To glorify God and enjoy him for ever'. A contrast is often made with the beginning of the catechism more frequently used in the Church of England: 'What is your name?'.

12 PP 260 (goal); 265 (lawyer's fantasy).

13 Analytical thinking PP 27 and 161–2; nice, unregenerate PP 84; see also TMHS 273 in which Sebastian describes his relatives as 'simultaneously the beams and the dry rot' and goes on to say that it was 'thanks to their goodness that the system was fundamentally insane – so insane that Susan's three charming children would almost certainly grow up to become cannon fodder'.

14 PP 80 (Traherne); see also 192. I am indebted to remarks once made at a Church conference in Northern Ireland by my erstwhile colleague J. J. Pritchard, Professor of Anatomy at The Queen's University of Belfast, to the effect that it was everyone's 'right' to walk around feeling 'absolutely marvellous'; and that thinkers such as Pascal, Kierkegaard and Sartre were generalizing from their own sickness. The Huxley of PP would have agreed with his initial statement; the author of DWYW would have heartily endorsed the second.

Chapter 7

1 AMS 217 – see I Kings, 1, 2–4; Jeremy's accent AMS 4; Huxley's, *Letters*, 609.

2 AMS 102 (dog/wolf); 312 (foetal ape); 237 (triturated viscera). For Sir Julian Huxley's reflections on carp, and a possible source for AMS, see Clark, *op. cit.*, 296.

3 AMS 257.

4 Fundamental All-rightness – AA 71, *Letters*, 779 and Huxley's last work, the essay on Shakespeare, published in MV 165–75, pp. 165–6, where he writes that 'a sense of the blessed All-Rightness of the Universe is a religious experience and so is the sick soul's sense of self-loathing, of despair, of sin, in a world that is the scene of perpetual perishing and inevitable death'; de Sade – AMS 78; and for Huxley's mistake, see Geoffrey Gorer, *The Life and Work of the Marquis de Sade*, Peter Owen, 1953, pp. 74 and 238.

5 See Russell, *op. cit.*, p. 267; for Dr Obispo's attitude, AMS 198, 266; science defined in TMHS 75.

6 See *Verses and a Comedy*, Chatto and Windus, 1946, p. 28. The poem is omitted from the 1970 edition of Huxley's *Collected Poetry*. Hidden God – see Isaiah, XLV, 15. In 1954 the late Lucien Goldmann wrote a study of Pascal and Racine to which he gave the title of *Le Dieu Caché*. Critics both in France and England took his neo-Marxist thesis quite seriously. But see P. Thody, *The Cosmic Pessimism of Hilaire Belloc, University of Leeds Review*, May 1970, and *Jeeves, Dostoievski and the Double Paradox*, *idem.*, October 1971 for a stricter application of his theories. Huxley's comment on the Pascal *pensée* Lafuma 418 to the effect that 'We might be reading a treatise, mercifully abbreviated, by Kant' also expresses in ten words the secondary thesis of Monsieur Goldmann's book. Increasing turpitude – AMS 195; parallel between Joe Stoyte and the Fifth Earl, 80 and 215. For a more comic dismissal of modern business, see the plot of AH, which revolves round the invention by Theodore Gumbril of 'patent small clothes': garments with inflatable rubber cushions sewn into them.

7 *op. cit.*, 29.

8 TMHS 188, 263. The politician Caccaguida, assures John Barnack in 1929 that Mussolini definitely has cancer of the throat.

9 See *Writers at Work, loc. cit.*, p. 172.

10 *Letters*, 482; PCP 544.

11 *op. cit.*, p. 3.

12 TMHS 257. For Huxley's views on reincarnation, see PP 41 and 176–7. Kierkegaard – see *Training in Christianity*, trans. Lowrie (O.U.P., p. 67, and p. 137.) Charm of birching – TMHS 159, 224. See also AMS 233 'Draconian birchings of the younger maids'. See also TMHS 102–3 for Eustace's tendency towards masochistic infantilism in sexual matters. 'Despairing insatiability' – TMHS 221. *Era tanto buono* – TMHS 196; Sybille Bedford in MV 141.

Chapter 8

1 TMHS best novel and not congenital novelist – see *Writers at Work, loc. cit.*, 172; and *Letters*, 680. Geoffrey Gorer – *Encounter*, July 1962, pp. 83–6. '*Island* is only technically a novel; it is basically a Utopia, designed by one of the most intelligent of living men.' The essay on Tibet is reprinted from *On the Margin* (1923) in the Everyman edition of *Stories, Essays and Poems*, pp. 275–7. Piero della Francesca – AR 181; Faraday – AR 224.

2 The essay is reprinted in *The Olive Tree*, 1936. See CW 1960, pp. 46–82.

3 *Letters*, 493 and 513. Huxley develops Sheldon's ideas more fully in PP 169–84, speaking particularly of Confucianism (182) as an 'amiably viscerotonic epicureanism (it would have suited Uncle Eustace and me), and of Christianity as perpetually threatened by a "somatotonic revolution" which tempts it to take this world seriously'.

4 *The First Circle*.

5 Clark, *op. cit.*, 352.

6 Julian's advice, see Clark, *op. cit.*, 152; *Vulgarity in Literature* was published both as a separate pamphlet in 1930 and in *Music at Night* in 1931. Little Phil, PCP 334; Sebastian, TMHS 133 'voluptuously, he imagined himself a consenting Adonis'; Mark Staithes, EG 322–3. For Huxley's view of Racine, see DL 95 'the yet more strictly limited universe of Racine's heroines and the somewhat featureless males who serve as a pretext for their anguish'. *Tragedy and the Whole Truth* is in the Everyman edition of the *Stories, Essays and Poems* as well as in *Music at Night*.

7 AR 157; EM 243; BMB 150; see also AMS 151 'The things old Bernini could have done with a battery of projectors.'

8 AA 14.

9 GE 293.

10 GE 20, 24.

11 GE 135.

12 GE 299.

13 GE 299.

14 AMS 195; Gervas Huxley, *op. cit.*, p. 212.

15 DL 219, 275; 151 – see Montaigne's essay *De la cruauté*.

16 DL 246, 314, 135.

17 *Letters*, 914. Huxley also enjoyed reading John Whiting's play. See *Letters*, 896, 901.

Chapter 9

1 *Letters*, 538.

2 GG 43. See *Letters*, 831 for similarity with Lawrence.

3 *op. cit.*, 190.

4 GG 75–6. See also the references in note 12 to Chapter VII.

5 Laura Archera Huxley, *op. cit.*, 209–15, p. 217. EG 52.

6 *Letters*, 435–7; JP 266.

7 *Letters*, 624, 860; definitely for matrimony 610.

8 GG 37.

9 AE 129, PCP 80. Significant books AMS 122; AE 89. Spankings AE 117.

10 *Letters*, 443–4.

11 *op. cit.*, p. 131; Krishnamurti, *Letters*, 917–18.

12 *Writers at Work*, *loc. cit.*, 171; HH 120; DP 31. My friend and colleague Mike Barrett, Professor of Pharmacology at the University of Leeds, tells me that the word 'soma' was used in the United States to designate the drug which, in this country, has to be called 'corisoma'; and which is 'used for low back pain and soft tissue injuries, sprains and strains where pain can be associated with muscle spasm'. It is, as he remarks, rather a come-down.

13 DP 57; surivive as animal 63; less soil 53; psychedelic, *Letters*, 917–18; Humphrey Osmond, Clark, *op. cit.*, 348.

14 Quoted in Anthony Smith, *The Body*, Pelican 1970, p. 22. T. H. Huxley, letter to Darwin 20.2.71.

15 DP 48, 104, 116, 128.

16 DWYW 202; totally incomprehensible DP; *Letters*, 769.

17 One of the many virtues of Professor Grover Smith's edition of

Huxley's *Letters* is that he quotes the whole passage on pp. 735–6.

18 DP 59.

19 *Letters*, 832. Almost one hundred pages of Professor Grover Smith's edition of the letters are taken up with problems connected with the production of this play; Real Dough, *Letters*, 727.

20 RKO, *Letters*, 946 (see also 537); musical comedy – *Letters*, 809, 822.

21 *Letters*, 892; Pinker, 460. It may well be, of course, that Huxley received royalties directly from the sale of his books, and that Pinker never had much money belonging to him at any one time. (But, cf. *Letters* p. 446 in which the sum of £2564 is owing to Huxley from Pinker.) In *This Timeless Moment*, Laura Archera Huxley refers to an interview which Huxley gave to the *Daily Mail* on his last visit to London, in 1962, and in which the sum of £250,000 was mentioned as the sum total of Huxley's literary earnings throughout his life.

22 Clark, *op. cit.*, p. 242; dirtiness – *Letters*, 625.

23 *Letters*, 795.

24 *This Timeless Moment*, 35, 117.

Chapter 10

1 *Letters*, 860.

2 *This Timeless Moment*, 193.

3 *Island*, 82, 84, 86.

4 *Island*, 93 (families), 99 (St Paul), 253 (God getting furious).

5 *Island*, 15, 150.

6 *Island*, 220.

7 *Island*, 117, Dr MacPhail – BMB 39. T. H. Huxley's book on Hume was published in 1879 in the English Men of Letters series (Macmillan).

8 *Island*, 127, 135–6.

9 See *The Reef* from *The Burning Wheel* (1916). *Collected Poetry*, 1971, p. 53.

10 See Peter Fryer, *The Birth Controllers*, Secker and Warburg, 1965, p. 138.

11 *Island*, 138. It is Murugan's favourite reading, and Huxley replied to a query from Ian Parsons in January 1962 (*Letters*, 886) to the effect that the quotations were taken from the 1959 or 1960 edition. He also mentioned the report that Franklin D. Roosevelt was said to have 'advocated free distribution of S-R catalogues in Communist countries, to convert the inhabitants, not to Christianity, but Consumerism'.

12 *Island*, 274. Essential Horror 242, where Huxley also writes that 'only God can make a microcephalous idiot'.

13 *Island*, 218, see Laura Archera Huxley, *op. cit.*, p. 199.

14 MV 123. Alexander Henderson, *op. cit.*, p. 244.

15 *Letters*, 912; tax advice, 737.

16 Laura Archera Huxley, *op. cit.*, 305–8.

Bibliography

No student of Huxley's work can fail to recognize the immense contribution which Professor Grover Smith's edition of the *Letters of Aldous Huxley* (Chatto and Windus, 1969) has made to our understanding both of the man and his work. Of comparable value is Ronald C. Clark's *The Huxleys*, with its admirable placing of Huxley's work against the background of his life and family tradition.

Critical studies of Huxley's work are numerous. The ones I have found most valuable are Peter Bowering's *The novels of Aldous Huxley* (University of London, The Athlone Press, 1968) and John Atkins: *Aldous Huxley. A Literary Study* (John Calder, 1956). Equally interesting is Laurence Brander, *Aldous Huxley. A critical study* (Rupert Hart-Davis, 1970), with its thesis that Huxley's work should be studied in the context of Ortega y Gasset's emphasis, in *The Revolt of the Masses*, on the change wrought in intellectual matters by the advent of the masses to full political power. The works of Aldous Huxley include:

Volumes marked with an asterisk * are available in Penguin books.

Limbo (short stories), 1920.
*Crome Yellow (novel), 1921.
*Mortal Coils (short stories), 1922.
On the margin (essays), 1923.
*Antic Hay (novel), 1923.
Little Mexican (short stories), 1924.
*Those Barren Leaves (novel), 1925.
Along the Road (travel), 1925.
Two or Three Graces (short novel), 1926.
Jesting Pilate (travel), 1926.
Proper Studies (essays), 1927.
*Point Counter Point (novel), 1928.
Do What You Will (essays), 1929.
This way to paradise (play; based upon *Point Counter Point*), 1930.
*Brief Candles (short stories), 1930.
The World of Light (play), 1931.
*Music at Night (essays), 1931.
*Brave New World (novel), 1932.
Texts and Pretexts (essays), 1932.
Beyond the Mexique Bay (travel), 1934.
*Eyeless in Gaza (novel), 1936.
The Olive Tree (essays), 1936.
An Encyclopedia of Pacifism, 1937.
Ends and Means. An Enquiry into the Nature of Ideals and into the Methods employed for their Realization (essays), 1937.
*After Many a Summer (novel), 1939.

Grey Eminence. A study in religion and politics (historical biography), 1941.
The Art of Seeing (essay), 1942.
*Time Must Have a Stop (novel), 1945.
The Perennial Philosophy (quotations with extended commentary), 1946.
Science, Liberty and Peace (essays), 1947.
Ape and Essence (novel in form of filmscript), 1948.
Themes and Variations (essays), 1950.
*The Devils of Loudun (historical biography), 1952.
*The Doors of Perception (essays), 1954.
The Genius and the Goddess (short novel), 1955.
*Heaven and Hell (essay), 1956.
Adonis and the Alphabet (essays), 1956.
Brave New World Revisited (essays), 1958.
Collected Short Stories, 1957.
*Island (novel), 1962.
Literature and Science (essays), 1962.

Index

Italicized figures indicate main entries